tea

Dear Imogen, Frank
and Honey,

Hope we share a
cuppa more often.

Love
Jacob, Molly & Sandra
x xoo

tea

A USER'S GUIDE

TONY GEBELY

Publication Date: October 2016

Editors: Melissa Caminneci and Lainie Petersen
Photography: Grant Komjakraphan
Layout & Cover Design: Sandra Friesen

Table of Contents

Introduction

This book is the result of my 10 years as a student of tea. Tea is one of those subjects where the more you learn, the less you know. Because of this, I vowed not to write this book in a vacuum. Rather, core ideas were shared with readers of World of Tea (www.worldoftea.org), and with the help of feedback I refined these ideas. Finer points were tested by extensive peer review.

Before we dive in, there is a bit of stage setting to do. This book isn't about *all* tea. It's about *specialty tea*. Specialty tea production prioritizes quality over quantity. Teas that fall beneath the *specialty* moniker exhibit a diversity in flavor that cannot be matched by coffee or even wine. Yet most of the world is only familiar with commodity tea—production that prioritizes quantity over quality. This is the cheap black tea (sold in individual tea bags) that most consumers know. The goal of this book is to celebrate the diversity of fresh, complex loose-leaf specialty teas.

You'll also notice that there are very few mentions of tea culture within this reference. Early on while writing this manuscript, I realized that by separating tea culture from objective tea study, we are left with a much better framework for tea education. It's much easier to learn about the tea itself and add color with culture later. This is a book about tea and only tea; there aren't any mythical stories, lengthy descriptions of preparation methods or even recipes for cooking with tea. This book strictly covers the journey of tea leaves from the field to the cup. I hope that you'll use it as a reference throughout your tea journey.

How to Use This Book

In this book you'll learn how tea is grown, harvested and processed into different tea types. You will also learn how to prepare tea properly at home; you'll gain a foundation of knowledge that will allow you to steep any tea and achieve desirable results.

In part one, we'll discuss the chemical properties of tea as it is propagated, harvested and processed. In part two we'll classify tea into six categories, building on information learned in part one. In part three we'll get to tea preparation and evaluation, the most important part of our tea journey.

Before we begin with part one, I want to give you an overview of my classification methods. The following pages also serve as an introduction to the romanized names that we'll be using in the book.

A LUMPER VIEW OF CLASSIFICATION

In any discipline that requires placing things into categories, there are generalists and specialists. I like to call these two factions *lumpers* and *splitters*. In general, lumpers prioritize similarities over differences and splitters prioritize differences over similarities. Tea snobs thrive on the splitter mentality; they point out differences in things in order to make themselves feel smarter than the average person. Splitters love to say things like "it's more complicated than this!" or "there are no absolutes in tea!" And while they may be right, I don't believe that the splitter mindset has any place in a beginner's tea education.

The content in this book represents a *lumper* view of tea classification. We will be working with seven main categories of tea, each defined by the unique steps they go through in processing. There is much more to be learned after understanding these general categories, but I caution the curious reader to not lose the real beauty of tea by becoming a tea snob. One of the most important parts of tea is the personal experience, and that's something that can't always be defined or learned.

ON PROPER ROMANIZATION

In the Western world, most tea terminology is badly romanized from Eastern Languages. I have taken great care to use standard Romanization methods to transliterate tea terms in this book. *Romanization* refers to the transliteration of any writing system to the Roman alphabet.

It is important to understand the difference between transliteration and translation. Transliteration tells us how to say the other language's word using our own writing system. Translation gives us a word in our own language that means the same thing as the other language's word.

Most words used in the tea industry today were romanized in one of three ways:

1. They were properly romanized via a standard romanization system
2. They were romanized using older, non-standard romanization systems
3. They were haphazardly transliterated by traders before romanization systems were in place, often from local dialects

Chinese, Japanese and Korean are languages made up of characters that represent a mix of ideas and spoken syllables, and we romanize these languages by expressing the spoken syllables with the Roman alphabet (our ABCs). Let's take 茶 as an example, the Chinese and Japanese character that translates to *tea* in English: that translation is not an accurate transliteration! The vast majority of Asian cultures do not pronounce the word that way; the Mandarin pronunciation of 茶 in the Roman alphabet is actually *cha*.

Then where did the word *tea* come from? You may notice that a bunch of languages have words for 茶 that sound like *cha* and a bunch of languages have words for 茶 that sound like *tea*. That is because there are many dialects of Chinese; *te* is the pronunciation of *cha* in Southern Fujian's Amoy dialect. It is believed that early Dutch and English tea traders wrote down what they heard in their own language, giving us *tea*. So 茶 translates to *tea* in English due to bad romanization of a particular dialect in the past, even though the generally accepted transliteration is *cha*.

THE WORD *TEA* IN MANY LANGUAGES

LANGUAGES WITH CHA WORDS		LANGUAGES WITH TE WORDS	
Language	Word	Language	Word
Chinese	Chá	English	Tea
Hindi	Chāy	Spanish	Té
Arabic	Shay	Indonesian	The
Russian	Chay	French	Thé
Portuguese	Chá	German	Tee

Most Asian and Middle Eastern countries follow the word's original pronunciation, cha. The majority of European-influenced countries use the pronunciation English speakers are more familiar with, tea.[1]

ROMANIZATION SYSTEMS

Most variant spellings you see on tea packages are a result of inconsistent romanization. Even well-known tea brands fail at accurate romanization, and their mistakes make it harder for the average consumer to correctly identify teas. Each country and region has their own challenges regarding romanization, though it can be most difficult with Chinese names.

China

The Chinese standard for romanization is Hanyu Pinyin. Hanyu Pinyin became the international standard for romanization of Modern Standard Chinese in 1982; prior to 1982, Wade-Giles was the primary method of romanization. Even though Hanyu Pinyin is the de facto standard, there are still many terms that were haphazardly transliterated from local dialects or romanized via the Wade-Giles system still in use today. I use Pinyin exclusively in this book.

Taiwan

Hanyu Pinyin became the national standard for romanization of Modern Standard Chinese in Taiwan in 2009. Because this was a recent decision, Wade-Giles is still very prevalent there. In the interest of consistency, I will be romanizing Taiwanese tea names with the Pinyin system.

Japan

Though the Kunrei-shiki romanization methods are taught to schoolchildren today, the Modified-Hepburn system is still the recognized standard. The fact that Modernized-Hepburn is used by the government for the romanization of passports and road signs is a testament to its prevalence; I will be using the Hepburn system for Japanese tea names.

South Korea

Revised Romanization, or RR, is currently the most popular method of romanization present for Korean. The RR method is also sometimes called the MCT method, which stands for Ministry of Culture and Tourism.

COMMON TEA TERMS: HANYU PINYIN VS. WADE-GILES

A lot of the variance in spelling we see in the tea world can be attributed to the mixed usage of the Hanyu Pinyin system and the older Wade-Giles system for Chinese. Here are some of the common words where we still see a lot of Wade-Giles usage:

HOW HANYU PINYIN DIFFERS FROM WADE-GILES

HANYU PINYIN	WADE-GILES
dong ding	tung ting
tie guan yin	tieh kuan yin
long jing	lung ching
gong fu	kung fu
Puer	Puerh
qing xin	chin hsin
bi luo chun	pi lo chun

HAPHAZARD TRANSLITERATIONS

Even more confusion arises with the prevalence of haphazard transliterations. One of the most common examples of this is the word "oolong," which in Hanyu Pinyin is "wulong." Common but incorrect transliterations such as this are unlikely to go away. Here are some other common haphazardly transliterated words that are still prevalent today:

HAPHAZARD TRANSLITERATIONS AND THEIR PINYIN COUNTERPARTS

TRANSLITERATION	HANYU PINYIN
souchong	xiao zhong
lapsang souchong	zheng shan xiao zhong
keemun	qimen
oolong	wulong
bohea	wuyi
pouchong	bao zhong
hyson	xi chun
tea	cha

the basics

Camellia sinensis, the Tea Plant

chapter 1

Defining Tea

WHAT IS TEA?

Most people think that any beverage made by steeping plant matter in water is tea. But to be considered true tea, what's being steeped must come from a broad-leaf perennial evergreen plant called *Camellia sinensis*—the tea plant.

Any other plant material steeped in hot water is technically called a tisane. The word tisane is derived from the Greek word *ptisane*. Many tea merchants call tisanes *herbal tea*. This includes mint, chamomile, hibiscus, lemongrass, ginger, yerba maté, guayusa, rooibos, and many more. Simply put, if it isn't from the *Camellia sinensis* plant, it's not tea.

But what exactly does this word *tea* mean? You may have noticed that the word *tea* often refers to the plant, its leaves, and the beverage we make from the tea leaves. This is really confusing, especially if you are just embarking on your tea journey. So to keep things simple as we explore tea from the field to the cup, I'll refer to the leaves of the *Camellia sinensis* plant as the *tea flush* or *tea leaves,* I'll refer to tea leaves that have been processed and are ready to be steeped as *finished tea* or *made tea* and finally, I'll refer to the beverage we make from the leaves as *tea* or *tea liquor.*

So if all true tea comes from the same plant, you may be wondering why there are so many different kinds of tea on the market today. How can they all be so different? Distinct teas arise from every part of the tea process: Tea is made from a specific variety or cultivar of *Camellia sinensis,* developed from the care given to the plants as they grow, formed by the methods used to harvest the leaves, and engineered by processing steps the leaves undergo once harvested and the variations in these processing steps. Even the location the tea plants are grown in has an astounding effect on the finished tea.

chapter 2

Tea Growing & Harvesting

In the name *Camellia sinensis*, *Camellia* refers to the genus and *sinensis* refers to the species of plant. Variations within a species are further noted by variety and cultivar. There are two varieties of *Camellia sinensis* used for tea production: var. *sinensis* which is derived from the Latin word for China, and var. *assamica* which is derived from the Latin word for Assam. The *assamica* variety is known for its large leaves, its hardiness, and its ability to grow to heights of 3o feet or more. *Assamica* cultivars are grown widely in India, Sri Lanka and Kenya, where they are often used for the production of black tea. The *sinensis* variety is known for its smaller leaves, and its cultivars are propagated widely around China, Taiwan and Japan.[1]

Before we continue, it's important to understand a bit about plant propagation. Plants can either be propagated sexually from seeds or asexually using grafts or cuttings. When plants are propagated sexually, the child plants will have characteristics that are different from those of their parents. When plants are propagated asexually, the resulting plants will be identical clones of the mother plant. Because of the highly variable nature of plants propagated sexually (grown from seeds), seedlings are not a suitable method of propagation for commercial tea production. Instead, when a plant grown from a seed possesses characteristics deemed beneficial such as a certain taste, aroma, leaf size, level of disease resistance, yield or hardiness, the plant is selectively cloned via asexual propagation in order to preserve (and mass produce) these characteristics. This clone is then given a name; these asexually reproduced plants are known as *cultivars*. The word cultivar is simply a portmanteau of the words cultivated and variety.

Most of the tea plants being grown commercially today are cultivars derived from two varieties of *Camellia sinensis*: sinensis and assamica. Most tea producing regions have research stations that develop new tea cultivars for tea production.

HOW TEA IS GROWN

Cultivated tea plants can be pruned into many shapes and sizes, but the bulk of world tea production relies on the cultivation of small tea plants pruned into waist-high rows for ease of harvest. The magnitude of planting varies greatly from farm to farm, ranging from tea plantations wherein up to 5000 tea plants may be planted per acre to smaller tea fields where only two or three thousand plants may be planted. There are even smaller operations where only a few unpruned tea trees are being grown.

Tea plants grow best in regions where the temperature is around 65–77 degrees Fahrenheit, with humidity levels between 75% and 85% and an annual distributed rainfall amount between 72 and 100 inches.[2] Regardless of location, tea plants prefer "well-drained soils with good organic matter content, pH in the range of 5 and 5.8 and ideally, sandy loam soil."[3]

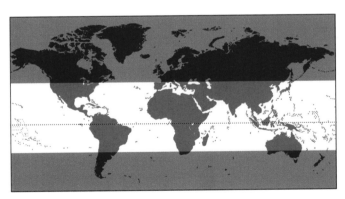

Where tea grows.

WHERE TEA IS GROWN

Camellia sinensis is a cultivated crop in over 49 countries between longitudes 42 degrees north and 33 degrees south.[4,5] It is often said that high elevation is required to grow good tea, but the climate is more beneficial than the elevation. Typical conditions at high elevations—cool air, clouds, and mist—slow the growth of the tea plant and produce tastier teas.

The majority of tea produced in the world is commodity tea, meaning that it is actively traded and its price is determined by the markets. Commodity tea is relatively cheap, with the worldwide average wholesale price of black tea typically in the area of $2.85/kilogram. This tea usually ends up in tea bags and in ready-to-drink (often referred to as *RTD*) tea beverages. Commodity tea is meant for the mass market. There is however, a larger amount of high quality tea being produced every year for the connoisseur market; some are calling this *specialty tea*.

HOW TEA LEAVES ARE HARVESTED

Under favorable conditions, it takes a tea plant 3–5 years to reach a point where it is mature enough to withstand being harvested. Plucking all of the leaves from a young tea plant would kill it; there must always be a base layer of foliage that is kept

A tea field.

TOP 25 TEA PRODUCING COUNTRIES[6]

RANK	COUNTRY	PRODUCTION (TONNES)
1	China, mainland	1924457
2	India	1208780
3	Kenya	432400
4	Sri Lanka	340230
5	Vietnam	214300
6	Turkey	212400
7	Iran	160000
8	Indonesia	148100
9	Argentina	105000
10	Japan	84800
11	Thailand	75000
12	Bangladesh	64000
13	Malawi	54000
14	Uganda	53000
15	Burundi	41817
16	United Republic of Tanzania	33700
17	Myanmar	31700
18	Mozambique	23000
19	Rwanda	22185
20	Nepal	20588
21	Zimbabwe	19000
22	Malaysia	18377
23	Ethiopia	7400
24	Cameroon	4700
25	Papua New Guinea	4700

intact. In India, this base layer of foliage is known as *maintenance foliage*. Maintenance foliage provides the energy the tea plant needs to continuously produce new shoots.

Before tea was commoditized, tea leaves were harvested from tea trees growing in the wild. If left to nature, an average tea plant would grow to be a tree 10–30 feet in height depending upon its growing conditions and the plant's variety. Obviously this isn't an ideal situation for harvesting leaves, so tea growers prune tea plants to about waist-high in order to provide a "plucking-table" from which to harvest shoots and leaves for processing. In some cases newly planted tea trees are allowed to grow unpruned, but this is only done on a limited scale to produce small batches of tea.

Under perfect conditions, where there is no cold season, tea plants can be harvested every ten days year-round. However, in most tea growing regions there *is* a cold season, and the plants generally yield no more than 6–7 harvests a year. Tea can be harvested by hand or by machine. Tea is best if harvested by hand because skilled workers are able to pluck only the leaves required for the style of tea being made. Hand-plucking results in less leaf breakage and allows more control over the final tea taste.

Darker maintenance foliage on tea plant.

Tea Fruit and Tea Flowers

Tea flowers and tea fruit appear on a tea plant when the plant is under stress. They are undesirable in tea production because they use up precious nutrients that could instead be going to the leaves that are used for making tea.

Hand Plucking and Plucking Standards

Whether tea is plucked by hand or harvested by machine is largely decided by labor costs and the quality of tea being made. It is not uncommon to see tea being handpicked even for cheap commodity tea. Nevertheless, picking tea leaves by hand is a very hard job. Skilled tea workers (usually women) generally pick for 6–8 hours a day, and they pluck anywhere from 5–15kg of tea a day depending on the type of tea leaves being plucked.

The number of leaves picked from the tea plant in a single plucking motion is called the *plucking standard.* Different finished tea styles require different plucking standards; anywhere from a single bud to a bud and several leaves are removed from the plant in a single pluck. Regardless of whether just buds, leaves, or a combination is plucked, the tea maker knows what plucking standard they need to make a specific style of tea. The tea leaves must be harvested at a very specific time of the plant's lifecycle.

Machine Harvesting

When harvesting by machine, it is often difficult to achieve a consistent cut of leaves. Tea harvesting machines basically act as lawn mowers that clip whatever is in their reach, resulting in a coarse, inconsistent product. This is problematic because consistency is key while processing tea leaves! When the tea leaves are cut in a coarse manner, chemical reactions within them occur at different rates. This results in inconsistent, sometimes harsh tasting tea. And once brewed, the varied particle sizes of the finished tea will steep at different rates.

As labor costs continue to rise worldwide, more attention is being given to machine harvesting. Some tea producing regions are using new pruning and field management techniques to produce better machine-harvested teas.

WHEN TEA LEAVES ARE HARVESTED

When tea leaves are harvested depends largely on the region in which they are being grown. The tea season can vary with fluctuations in weather. The timing of the harvest is of utmost importance, as missing the harvest can destroy a crop. It can take only a few days for a bud to appear, open up and mature.

Each growing region has special terminology for referring to their tea harvest periods. In India and Nepal, each harvest is called a *flush*, a term that refers

A flushing tea plant: notice the row of plants on the right and their lighter colored "flush" of new leaves.

to a period of growth in the tea plant. In China, Taiwan and South Korea, the terms used to denote tea harvests relate to dates in the traditional East Asian lunisolar calendar.

When there is a dormancy period due to cool weather (usually winter) in the tea field, the first new shoots after this period are said to be of the highest quality because they have been building up nutrient reserves over the dormancy period to produce the new leaves. Because of this, the first harvest of each year is often the most sought after and usually the most expensive. Many growing regions have special names for this first harvest. In India and Nepal, it is called the *First Flush*. In China these teas are known as *Pre-Qing Ming* teas, in Japan they are referred to as *Shincha*, and in South Korea they are called *Ujeon*.

Here's a guide to the harvest seasons for the world's major producers of *specialty teas*: India, Nepal, China, Japan, South Korea and the countries of East Africa.

Darjeeling (India) and Nepal teas

The Darjeeling and Nepali harvest period lasts from late March to early November and is broken up into 4 parts: first flush, second flush, monsoon flush, and autumnal flush. At times, the plants will continue to flush past November; this is sometimes called a winter flush.

· First Flush: March – April
· Second Flush: May – June
· Monsoon Flush: July – August
· Autumnal Flush: October – November

Assam (India)

Like Darjeelings, Assams are typically harvested from March to December. Higher quality teas are harvested here during two distinct growth periods, the first and second flush. All other grades of tea are harvested after this period. The first flush begins in March, and the second flush begins in June.

Nilgiri (India) and Sri Lanka teas

Due to the warmth in the southernmost tropical growing regions of Nilgiri in South India and Sri Lanka, tea plants can be harvested year-round.

China

The harvest season in China varies greatly with the different growing regions and elevations there, but in general the harvest season can begin as early as March and can last until late November. Finished teas that are made from young leaves or buds have a more finite growing season and will often be harvested on specific dates on the East Asian lunisolar calendar. Teas plucked before Qing Ming (清明, *qīng míng*; literally "clear bright") are highly sought after and command a premium; these teas are called *Pre Qing Ming* or *Ming Qian* teas. Here are the two most highly regarded harvest seasons:

· Ming Qian (明前, *míng qián*; literally "before Qing Ming") tea harvested before Qing Ming festival which falls on April 4–6
· Yu Qian (雨前, *yǔ qián*; literally "before the rains") tea picked before the Grain Rain on April 20

Finished teas that are made from older leaves do not usually follow such a strict harvest calendar and can be harvested at any time from April to November. Wulong is an example of a tea that is made from older, more mature leaves and as such follows a less strict harvesting schedule. For many Wulongs, the most sought-after harvests begin in September and run through Autumn.

Japan

The harvest season in Japan varies by region as well, but it typically begins in late April and ends in early October. Japan's sought-after first harvest is called *Shincha*. Japan has four distinct harvest periods:

· Shincha (新茶: literally "new tea"): this is the name given to the first harvest of the year.
· Ichibancha (一番茶: literally "first tea") this refers to the entire first harvest season, including schincha. Typically occurs from late April to May.

- Nibancha (二番茶: literally "second tea") refers to the second harvest of the year, taking place from June to the end of July.
- Sanbancha (三番茶: literally "third tea") refers to the third harvest of the year taking place in August.
- Yonbancha (四番茶: literally "fourth tea") is the fourth harvest of the year; it can take place as late as October in some regions.

South Korea

South Korea's growing seasons correspond to dates on the lunisolar calendar. Finished tea from the first harvest of the year is called *Ujeon*. Harvest periods that follow Ujeon contain the root word *jak*, which comes from the word *jakseolcha or* "sparrow's tongue." This is a reference to tiny buds from the tea plant that resemble the tongue of a sparrow. It is important to know that different grades of tea are harvested during different times in South Korea.

- Ujeon (우전; literally "before the rain") refers to tea picked before April 20. This season corresponds to Gogu on the lunisolar calendar.
- Sejak (세작; literally "small sparrow") is tea picked before May 5–6. This corresponds to Ipha on the lunisolar calendar.
- Jungjak (중작; literally "medium sparrow") is tea picked around May 20–21. This corresponds to Soman on the lunisolar calendar.
- Daejak (대작; literally "large sparrow") refers to lower quality large leaves tea picked during summer.

Africa

In the East African tea producing countries of Kenya, Malawi, Mozambique, Uganda, Rwanda, Zimbabwe, Burundi, and Ethiopia, tea is harvested year round due to the lack of a cold season. Peak tea production coincides with the rainy seasons.

READY FOR PROCESSING

Once tea leaves are harvested, they are transported to the place where they will be processed. Some tea farms process tea on site, while other farms sell their tea leaves to central processing facilities responsible for processing leaves from many different farmers.

Before we get into how the leaves are processed into finished teas, let's look at the chemical composition of the leaves. An understanding of the chemicals inside tea leaves will help us understand the outcomes of processing.

chapter 3

Chemical Composition of Tea Leaves

Tea chemistry is complex. Just how complex? Well, on the bush, tea leaves contain thousands of chemical compounds. When tea leaves are processed, the chemical compounds within them break down, form complexes with one another and form new compounds. When steeping tea leaves, our senses are tingled by the thousands of volatile compounds (collectively known as the "aroma complex") rising from the tea liquor and the thousands of non-volatile compounds that are floating within the tea liquor. Because of this, tea is known as "the ultimate master of chemical diversity."[1] Much of tea chemistry from field to cup is yet unknown!

So all of this makes it very difficult to generalize and say that x chemical is responsible for y taste. Many tea chemicals have been categorized into broad groups, and collectively we have some idea of what happens to these groups during processing and what flavors and aromas they are responsible for. Undoubtedly, as tea gains popularity, more research will be done on tea chemistry and we'll have a clearer picture of what is going on chemically from the field to the cup.

Plant leaves are made up of mostly water, and they begin to wilt and lose water when they are removed from the plant. Tea leaves are no exception to this. Once they are plucked, the leaves begin to lose water and wilt, a process called *withering* in the tea industry. As tea leaves wither, their cell walls begin to break down. The chemical components inside come in contact with oxygen, spurring on a group of reactions we call *oxidation*. Over the years, tea producers have learned to control the natural tendency of tea leaves to wither and oxidize in order to produce a finished tea that has a desirable appearance, aroma and taste. This is accomplished using methods we'll refer to as *tea processing*.

Amazingly, for hundreds of years tea makers have produced drinkable teas using principles of withering and oxidation with no knowledge of the underlying chemistry. From what we know today, the most important compounds in fresh tea leaves are polyphenols, amino acids, enzymes, pigments, carbohydrates, methylxanthines, minerals and many volatile flavor and aroma compounds. These components are responsible for producing teas with desirable appearance, aroma, and taste. During tea processing the various compounds undergo changes to produce what we'll call a *finished* or *made* tea – one that has been processed and is ready for packaging or steeping.

Let's take a look at each of these compounds, beginning with the most abundant, polyphenols.

POLYPHENOLS

In steeped teas, polyphenols are largely responsible for astringency, a taste experience that causes a drying sensation on the tongue and bitterness. The term *polyphenol* simply refers to a categorization of compounds composed of many phenolic groups, hence the name *poly-phenol*. These compounds are plant metabolites produced as a defense against insects and other animals, and they are the most abundant compounds in tea. Polyphenols comprise as much as 30–40% of freshly plucked tea leaves[2] and solids in tea liquor.[3] Polyphenols are derived from amino acids via sunlight, and therefore tea grown in the shade has a smaller concentration of polyphenols and a higher concentration of amino acids.[4] The bud and first leaf have the highest concentration of polyphenols, and polyphenol levels decrease in each leaf moving down the plant.[5] There are an estimated 30,000 polyphenolic compounds in tea.[6] There are several known categories within polyphenols. Flavonoids are arguably the most important category; they are the reason for many health claims surrounding tea because they contain antioxidants.

Within the flavonoid group are flavanols, flavonols, flavones, isoflavones, and anthocyanins. Flavanols (short for flavan-3-ols) are the most prevalent and thus the most studied. Flavanols are often referred to as *tannins* or *catechins*. The major flavanols in tea are: catechin (C), epicatechin (EC), epicatechin gallate (ECG), gallocatechin (GC), epigallocatechin (EGC), and epigallocatechin gallate (EGCG). EGCG is the most active of the catechins, and this flavanol is often the subject of studies regarding tea antioxidants.

Flavanols are converted to theaflavins and thearubigins during oxidation. They are the compounds responsible for the dark color and robust flavors that are present in oxidized teas.

Flavonols, flavones, isoflavones and anthocyanins are thought to contribute to the color of a tea's infusion and its taste.

AMINO ACIDS

Amino acids give finished tea its sweetness and brothiness, otherwise known as *umami*. In the tea field, sunlight converts amino acids to polyphenols; shade-grown tea contains more amino acids than tea grown in direct sunlight. Some tea bushes are even deliberately shaded for several weeks before harvest to increase the amino acid content in the leaves, a process that results in finished tea with strong umami. Tea plants that are shaded for 22 days contain 4 times more amino acids than non-shaded plants.[7]

Tea leaves contain many amino acids, the most abundant of which is *theanine*. Theanine, specifically L-Theanine, is responsible for promoting alpha brain wave activity and a feeling of relaxation. L-Theanine in concert with caffeine can induce a state of "mindful alertness" in the tea drinker. Amino acids make up an average of 6% of the extract solids in steeped tea.[8]

L-Theanine in Nature

Camellia sinensis, a mushroom called *Boletus badius*, and a plant called *Guayusa* (which is often processed as a tisane) are the only three known natural sources of theanine in nature.

ENZYMES

Polyphenol oxidase and peroxidase are the most important enzymes in tea leaves. They are responsible for the enzymatic browning of tea leaves that takes place when the cell walls in the leaves are broken and the polyphenols are exposed to oxygen – otherwise known as *oxidation*. These same enzymes are responsible for the browning of apples, potatoes, avocados and bananas. Polyphenol oxidase and peroxidase may be denatured or deactivated using heat so that browning cannot occur. In fact, this is one of the first steps in green tea production; it is why finished green tea leaves remain green (and why cooked apples or potatoes remain white). Polyphenol oxidase and peroxidase are deactivated and thus rendered inactive at around 150 degrees Fahrenheit. The enzymes may also be deactivated by simply depriving them of moisture for a time; this is what happens during the long withering period in white tea production.

PIGMENTS

Plant pigments give leaves their color and are responsible for absorbing light for photosynthesis. There are two major groups of pigments in fresh tea leaves: *chlorophylls* and *carotenoids*. These pigments condense during withering and oxidation, causing them to become darker. During oxidation, green chlorophylls degrade and become black pigments known as *pheophytins*. This degradation leads to the dark appearance of finished oxidized teas. Tea *carotenoids*, another pigment group found in tea leaves, can be characterized into two smaller groups: orange *carotenes* and yellow *xanthophylls*.

During processing, carotenoids degrade into many derivative compounds that provide flavor in the cup. The most important and widely studied of these compounds is damascenone, which lends itself to the sweetness of a finished tea.[9] Because carotenoid levels decline during oxidation and are higher in more mature leaves often used in wulong production, wulongs contain the highest amounts of demascenone.

CARBOHYDRATES

All plants store energy formed during photosynthesis in starches and sugars, otherwise known as carbohydrates. Plants later use this stored energy to fuel important reactions. In tea, carbohydrates help fuel the enzymatic reactions that take place during oxidation and are also responsible for the creation of polyphenols in young tea leaves.[10] Carbohydrates make up on average 11% of extract solids in steeped tea[11] and consist of monosaccharides, disaccharides and oligosaccharides.[12] These carbohydrates lend to the sweetness of the tea liquor.

METHYLXANTHINES

The main Methylxanthine in tea is the stimulant caffeine. Other methylxanthines found in tea are two chemically similar compounds, theobromine and theophylline. The tea plant creates these chemicals as a way to ward off insects and other animals. On average, methylxanthines make up 2% to 5% of the dry weight of the fresh tea leaves.[13] Methylxanthines also contribute to a bitter taste in the tea infusion. The level of methylxanthines in tea depends on the variety and cultivar of *Camellia sinensis* used, the climate, the age of the leaves, and the propagation method (seed vs. cutting) used on the plant.

MINERALS

28 mineral elements have been found in tea leaves.[14] Compared to other plants, tea contains high amounts of fluorine, manganese, arsenic, nickel, selenium, iodine, aluminum, and potassium.[15] Of these minerals, fluorine is the most studied. Fluorine, often used to prevent tooth decay in humans, can cause fluorosis if high levels are consumed.[16] The abundance of minerals in a tea flush varies greatly with each harvest, and their levels can also change greatly during processing.

VOLATILES

Volatile substances easily enter the air from tea leaves or tea liquor, and they reach our olfactory system as a vapor. Thus, volatile substances are largely responsible for the drink's flavor and aroma. This is remarkable considering that volatile substances make up only about 0.01% of the weight of dry tea leaves.[17]

Tea's *aroma complex* is made up of hundreds (maybe even thousands) of volatile flavor and aroma compounds that exist in trace amounts. Many of these aromatic compounds do not exist in fresh tea leaves; they are instead derived from other substances during processing. The aroma complex is sometimes broken into two parts: primary aroma (from fresh tea leaves) and secondary aroma (products of processing). The flavor and aroma of each finished tea depends on a wide variety of combinations of compounds, hence the name *aroma complex*. Compounds such as linalool and linalool oxide are responsible for floral notes and sweetness; geraniol and phenylacetaldehyde are responsible for floral aromas; nerolidol, benzaldehyde, methyl salicylate, and phenyl ethanol are responsible for fruity flavors; and trans-2-hexenal, n-hexanal, cis-3-hexenol, and b-ionone are responsible for a tea's fresh flavor.[18] More and more research is being done on tea volatiles and how our olfaction system works in general, so we may expect some clarity on tea volatiles in the coming years.

chapter 4

Tea Processing

Welcome to the tea processing chapter; this is where the magic happens! In this chapter we'll explore how the chemical compounds found in tea leaves are transformed to produce teas with desirable appearance, aroma, and taste. Tea processing has the most influence on finished tea, and the steps taken during processing are responsible for determining what type of tea is being created.

The major steps in tea processing are withering, oxidation (or lack thereof), drying and sorting. As we discussed in the last chapter, once tea leaves are removed from the plant they begin to wilt and lose water, a process we call *withering*. As tea leaves wither, their cell walls begin to break down and *oxidation* begins. Tea processing refers to the steps taken to control the natural tendency of tea leaves to wither and oxidize. Let's discuss each of these processes in detail, beginning with withering.

WITHERING

We have discussed the fact that the moment a tea leaf is plucked from the tea plant, it begins to wilt naturally, a process we call *withering*. But once the tea leaves reach the processing facility, this process is controlled by the tea producer. The purpose of a controlled wither is to prepare the leaves for further processing by reducing their moisture content. This allows for the development of aroma and flavor compounds in the leaves. Controlling the withering process means closely monitoring humidity, temperature and air-flow over time. A controlled wither can occur outside with tea leaves laid out gently on bamboo mats or tarps, or indoors in troughs with forced air. The air may be heated to speed up the process if necessary.

Great care is also given to the density of the withering leaves to ensure that they wither evenly. The withering process is complete once the tea leaves have achieved a desired percentage of water loss. This is determined by the final weight of the tea leaves after withering or by the flaccidity and changes in the aroma of the leaves.

During withering, the moisture content in the leaf is reduced by about one-third to one-half, making the leaf flaccid and pliable. This prepares the leaf for further processing, including shaping and rolling. On the chemical side of things, chlorophyll in the leaf begins to degrade, caffeine levels slowly rise, flavor and aroma volatiles develop in the leaves and grassy aromas dissipate.[1] Since the leaves are cut off from their supply of energy, they also begin to break down their stored carbohydrates for use as energy. The loss of moisture also causes the cell walls to break down, initiating polyphenol oxidase and peroxidase activity – otherwise known as oxidation.

The longer the wither endures, the more new aroma and flavor compounds develop in the leaves. This is because during the withering process, many of the chemical compounds in the leaves degrade into volatile compounds. In fact, many tea makers use their sense of smell to tell when the withering process is complete. If the leaves are withered too long, polyphenol and peroxidase activity will cease due to dehydration. Once withering is deemed complete, processing continues.

OXIDATION

Oxidation refers to a series of chemical reactions that result in the browning of tea leaves and the production of flavor and aroma compounds in finished teas. Depending on the type of tea being made, oxidation is either prevented altogether or deliberately initiated, controlled and then stopped.

Much of the oxidation process revolves around polyphenols, particularly the enzymes polyphenol oxidase and peroxidase. When the cells inside tea leaves are damaged and the components inside mix and are exposed to oxygen,[2] a chemical reaction begins. This reaction converts the polyphenols known as catechins into flavanoids called theaflavins and thearubigins (which are also polyphenols). Theaflavins provide tea with its briskness and bright taste as well as its yellow color,[3] and thearubigins provide tea with depth, body and its reddish color.[4] Chlorophylls are converted to pheophytins and pheophorbides (pigments that lend to the black/brown color of dry oxidized tea leaves) during oxidation, and lipids, amino acids and carotenoids degrade to produce some of tea's flavor and aroma compounds. Tea producers use special methods to initiate, halt (fix), or even prevent oxidation in order to produce different flavors in a finished tea.

Initiation

Oxidation begins when the cell walls within tea leaves are damaged. To achieve cell damage, tea producers macerate, roll or tumble tea leaves to intentionally initiate oxidation. Maceration is the quickest path to full oxidation because the insides of the leaves are immediately exposed to oxygen, resulting in a greater mixture of the chemicals within.

Maceration is typically used in mass production methods to create CTC (cut tear curl) tea or other broken leaf teas. The process is achieved using a rotorvane or a CTC machine. Rolling results in a much slower and gentler oxidation, and it is usually done using a rolling table or by hand. Tumbling is an even gentler way to initiate oxidation, and it is achieved using large cylinders wherein the leaves are tumbled or by hand-shaking the leaves on top of a shallow bamboo basket. Regardless of the method of initiation, great care must be taken up to this point as any damage to the leaves before processing will cause premature oxidation and result in an unevenly processed finished tea.

Control

Control over oxidation is maintained by introducing warm, moist, oxygen-rich air over time. The extent to which oxidation is allowed to occur has an astounding effect on the finished tea. Oxidation occurs best between 80–85 °F and is slowed nearly to a halt at 140–150 °F.[5] Thus, when the tea producer wishes to halt oxidation, they heat the leaves. This heating process is known as *fixing*.

Fixing

Fixing works by denaturing polyphenol oxidase and peroxidase – the enzymes primarily responsible for oxidation using heat. Fixing is also commonly referred to as *de-enzyming*,[6] *denaturing* or *kill-green*.

The term *kill-green* is derived from the Chinese term *shaqing* (杀青), which translates to *killing the green*. The tea leaves must be heated to approximately 150 degrees Fahrenheit to "halt" oxidation. Oxidation is further slowed by drying the leaves, but it never *completely* stops. At temperatures over 150 degrees Fahrenheit, oxidation continues to occur at an extremely slow pace. The process of fixing requires precise control of the temperature and length of heating; each has to be adjusted depending on the size and thickness of the leaves and the amount being processed.

Most common fixing methods:

· Pan Firing: where tea leaves are heated in a large metal pan or wok that is heated by gas or wood fire[7]
· Steaming: where steam is forced through the mass of tea leaves[8]
· Tumblers: where a heated tumbler is used to heat the leaves[9]
· Baking: where an oven type machine is used to heat the leaves[10]

Less common fixing methods:

- Sun drying: where the heat of the sun denatures the enzymes in the leaf by dehydration
- Microwaving: where electromagnetic waves are used to quickly heat the leaves, seen more in commercial applications
- Plunging in boiling water: where tea leaves are literally plunged into boiling water

When oxidation is prevented altogether, the catechins are left largely intact. The tea leaves keep their green color and vegetal characteristics. Think of an apple: once it is sliced open it quickly turns brown, but the apples in apple pie are not brown. This is because the heat used to bake the pie denatured the polyphenol oxidase and peroxidase in the apples and prevented enzymatic browning. The same browning effect takes place in potatoes, avocados, bananas, etc.

When a semi-oxidized tea is being produced, some catechins convert to theaflavins and thearubigins, resulting in a slight browning usually along the edges of the leaves and yellower liquor. Lipids, amino acids, and carotenoids also begin to break down into flavor and aroma compounds.

When oxidation is allowed to run its course, the leaves exhibit an aroma and taste profile completely unrecognizable from a finished tea that was exempted from oxidation. Theaflavins and thearubigins will now outnumber catechins, resulting in a brisk tasting tea with a reddish color in the cup. The chlorophylls will have been converted to pheophytins and pheophorbides, turning the leaves a coppery brown, and a myriad of new volatiles will have developed. In this case, the leaves are often just dried to halt any still-occurring reactions and to bring the tea to a shelf-stable moisture level. This is a bit of a grey area in tea processing because here, drying can be considered a form of fixing. Heat is being used and oxidation is being halted. This is a great example of why it is sometimes important to view tea processing as more of a continuum rather than as a distinct set of steps. Regardless, there's more to drying we need to look into.

DRYING
In all of our talk of tea processing thus far, we've been dealing with tea leaves that contain some water. In order for processed tea leaves to be shelf-stable,[11] they must be dried. Drying both makes the tea leaves shelf stable and enhances their flavor. At times, these can be two distinct steps in processing; at other times, it can be seen as more of a continuum. Sometimes teas are only dried for shelf-stability. For our discussion here, I'll explain each separately.

Most common drying methods:
- Commercial dryers: perforated conveyors move the tea leaves through a heat source in an endless chain. Leaves can also be moved through fluidized bed dryers and dried on a bed of hot air.
- Oven drying: tea leaves are set on perforated trays in an oven and hot air is circulated through the tea via convection.
- Sun drying: tea leaves are spread outdoors (usually on shallow bamboo baskets) to dry in the sun.

Less common drying methods:

· Charcoal firing: tea leaves set in a shallow bamboo basket are heated slowly over hot coals.
· Drying on a heated floor: tea leaves are dried on a thick masonry floor heated from below.[12]

Drying for Shelf Stability

Drying for stability means reducing the moisture level in the tea leaves to 2–3%. Doing so makes the leaves shelf-stable and slows the oxidative processes within the leaves to nearly a full stop. Tea makers control the temperature of the air, the volume of air moving past the tea, and the amount of time that drying occurs to produce a palatable tea. Drying the tea too slowly results in stewing, and drying it too quickly results in the outside of the leaves drying much quicker than the inside, a condition known in tea production as *case hardening*. According to India's Tocklai Tea Research Institute, "an average loss of more than 4% moisture per minute leads to bitterness and harshness in made tea. Moisture loss at 2.8–3.6% per minute has been found to produce teas with good quality."[13]

Drying for Flavor Enhancement

Drying for flavor enhancement refers to two optional processing methods known as finish-firing and roasting. Both involve heat, and both can be seen as distinct processing steps or part of drying for shelf-stability. Not all teas are finish-fired or roasted; typically these processes are reserved for higher-end teas and are skipped in commercial tea production. This type of drying alters the taste via the pyrolysis of the amino acids and sugars in the tea leaves.[14]

Finish-firing refers to a very low temperature heating of tea leaves for several hours, typically in an oven or in shallow bamboo baskets over hot coals. After the leaves cool, they are immediately packed and shipped. This enhances the flavor and aroma of the leaves but doesn't necessarily change it.

Roasting, on the other hand refers to a method of heating that is meant to change the flavor and aroma of the tea, typically adding toasty, burnt notes and resulting in a darker tea and a darker infusion depending upon how long the tea is roasted and at what temperature. Roasting also occurs in an oven or in shallow bamboo baskets over hot coals.

SORTING

The last step in tea production is sorting. Sorting includes cleaning and sifting tea leaves. Commodity teas are sorted by machines where vibrating conveyors with differing mesh sizes are used to sift tea leaves into different particle sizes and grades of tea. Everything from tea dust and fannings to broken leaves and whole leaves are separated and sold as different grades of tea. For higher end teas, sorting is usually done by hand.

tea classification

chapter 5

Tea Types

WHY CLASSIFY?

The goal of tea classification is to provide a clear foundation for education and evaluation by grouping together teas with similar qualities. Throughout history, tea has been classified many ways, including:

· Classification by the color of the finished tea leaves
· Classification by the color of the tea liquor
· Classification by the percentage of oxidation the tea leaves have gone through during processing

Each of these methods fall short of providing a method by which all teas can be categorized.

It is better to classify teas by the processing methods that created them; nearly all teas can easily be lumped together by similarities in the processing steps they undergo. The tea classification chart below represents the minimum level of processing a tea must go through to be considered an archetype of a specific tea category.

TEA PROCESSING CHART

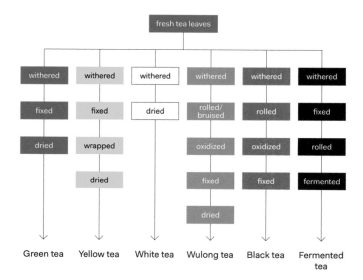

New tea styles occasionally arise that threaten tea categories, and at times, differences between tea processing steps should be seen as more of a continuum rather than distinct steps. Nonetheless, it is important to learn how these steps affect the outcome of a tea and the creation of different types of tea.

SEVEN TYPES OF TEA

Because nearly all tea processing methods in use today are derived from Chinese techniques, it makes sense to begin our study of classification in China. Most Chinese tea experts recognize the following six tea types:

- *Green Tea* (绿茶, *lǜ chá*)
- *Yellow Tea* (黄茶, *huáng chá*)
- *White Tea* (白茶, *bái chá*)
- *Wulong Tea* (乌龙茶, *wū lóng chá*)
- *Red Tea* (红茶, *hóng chá*)
- *Dark Tea* (黑茶, *hēi chá*).

There are two major differences when comparing the Chinese classification to most Western classification systems. You may not be familiar with the terms *red tea* and *dark tea.*

Red tea is the translation of the Mandarin hong cha (红茶, *hóng chá*) which refers to what most Westerners call *black tea*. The Chinese named this tea after the reddish color of the tea's liquor, whereas the Western world derives their name for this tea from the typical black color of the finished tea's leaves. Calling this tea category *black tea* is confusing when dealing with Chinese tea leaves, because the Chinese already have a tea category called hei cha (黑茶, *hēi chá*) that translates to *black* or *dark tea.*

Dark tea refers to a category of fermented teas, again named after the color of the tea's liquor. Dark teas can be very dark, nearly black. The dark tea category includes Puer (普洱, *pǔěr*) as well as many other fermented teas.

Tea types by liquor color. From left to right: green tea, yellow tea, white tea, wulong tea, black tea, fermented tea

To avoid confusion for a Western audience, I refer to hong cha as *black tea* and hei cha as *fermented tea.*

In this book I've expanded upon the traditional Chinese classification systems to encapsulate nearly all teas regardless of origin. Hence, from fresh *Camellia sinensis* leaves, it is possible to derive seven types of tea via processing. These broad categories lump together types of tea that share similar processing methods and consequently, similar final products. In the chart above, six primary tea categories are represented: green tea, yellow tea, white tea, wulong tea, black tea, and fermented tea. But each of these six tea types can be altered by flavoring, scenting, blending, grinding, roasting, aging, decaffeination, and so on. These altered teas comprise a seventh category we'll refer to as *Altered Tea.*

HIERARCHY OF CLASSIFICATION OF FINISHED TEAS

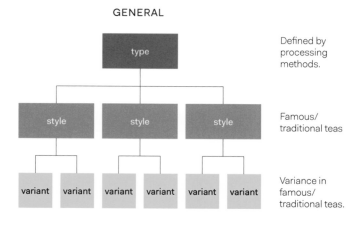

TEA STYLES

We now know that there are six primary tea *types* and a seventh category called Altered Tea, but this does not explain why there are so many *kinds* of tea on the market today (a lot more than seven!). These *kinds of tea* we'll call *styles*. Within each tea type category, there can be hundreds if not thousands of tea styles. What makes them unique are the:

- Variations in processing steps they've undergone
- The specific cultivar of the tea plant used
- Terroir (soil, climate, altitude, latitude)

In fact, some tea styles are not considered to be authentic unless they are made using very specific processing steps from a specific cultivar grown in a specific terroir. Let's explore the differentiating factors that make up a tea style in more detail.

Variations in Processing

Variations in processing (like steaming instead of pan firing for fixing, final percentage of oxidation, or different shaping methods) can dramatically affect the outcome of a tea, which is why certain variations can make up much of the definition of a tea style.

Some tea styles are named after the shape or color of the finished leaves, and some are named after the color or taste of the liquor. All of these factors are related to variations in the processing methods used to create them.

Cultivar

While we can technically create any type or style of tea from any cultivar of *Camellia sinensis*, the outcome may not be desirable or authentic. Many cultivars have been bred specifically for certain growing regions to be processed into a specific style of tea.

Some tea styles are even defined solely by their cultivar; in this case there is often a mother plant that has been cloned for commercial production. China's Tie Guan Yin and Tie Luo Han are two examples of these from the wulong category.

Terroir

Terroir, sometimes *Goût de terroir*, literally "taste of the earth" is a French term used to describe the taste imparted by the soil, climate, altitude, and latitude of a particular growing region. Some tea styles are named after the place in which they are grown, and others are only considered authentic if grown in a specific region.

VARIANTS

Tea *variants* come into play when discussing variations in a tea style. The word specifically refers to differences in husbandry practices, harvesting techniques and processing methods. Variations often define the difference between traditional tea production and commercial tea production. It is important to note that for nearly every tea style, there may be variations hand-made by artisans as well as variations mass produced by a factory on the market. This brings up the issue of quality.

Let's look at the differences in husbandry, harvesting, processing and terroir from a traditional versus commercial view:

DIFFERENCES IN TRADITIONAL AND COMMERCIAL PRODUCTION

	TRADITIONAL	COMMERCIAL
Husbandry	Possibly wild or planted from seed. No chemicals, not always in neat rows.	Pruned often, planted from cuttings. Use of chemicals, planted in neat rows.
Harvesting	By hand.	Mechanical methods.
Processing	Greater care in general. Usually smaller batches. Less reliance on machines.	Larger batches, possibly less attention and care given during processing. Complete reliance on machinery.
Withering	Outdoors; sometimes indoors under tarps.	Indoors in withering troughs with forced air.
Fixing	By hand in a pan over fire.	In a heated tumbler.
Rolling	By hand.	Mechanical methods.
Drying	Pan or basket-fired.	In an oven.

Variations in terroir also exist. For every tea style defined by its origin, there may be several variations of the same tea style made in a neighboring region. In tea circles, the question of authenticity often comes up regarding these regions. What makes a tea authentic? Is Puer from Guangdong Puer? Is Long Jing from Sichuan Long Jing? There really are no absolutes when it comes to tea styles and variations; these words are just tools that we use when describing and evaluating finished teas.

chapter 6

Green Tea

In one simple sentence, green tea is a type of tea made from leaves that have been withered, fixed and dried. The goal of green tea production is to preserve the natural polyphenols in the leaves by preventing oxidation. These processes serve to preserve the natural fresh taste of the tea plant; the best green tea is made from tender young leaves. The style of a green tea depends on any variations in these steps, the variety and cultivar of the plant being used, and its terroir. There are thousands of styles of green tea available on the market today.

Once tea leaves have been withered and fixed, they can easily be rolled or shaped. Tea leaves have been rolled and shaped for commercial use since China's early Ming Dynasty, around the time when the grinding of tea leaves fell out of style. The process of rolling and shaping tea leaves varies depending on tea style, and many times these processes involve special hand movements passed down over the generations. The shape of a finished tea depends largely on the plucking standard used for the tea. Today, while some teas are still being processed by hand, most teas are shaped by complex machines and rollers.

The Japanese are well-known for their production of *steamed ryokucha* (緑茶), literally *green tea.* Steaming here is the method of fixing used to halt oxidation during processing. Japan's most notable steamed green teas are sencha, kabusecha, gyokuro, and the powdered tea matcha. In fact, nearly 98% of all tea produced in Japan is steamed green tea. 42% of Japanese green tea production comes from Shizuoka Prefecture and 18% comes from Kagoshima Prefecture.[1]

The length of time the leaves are steamed is very important; this one factor can dramatically affect the outcome of the tea. There are several Japanese words used to denote the length of time that the leaves are steamed. The word mushi (蒸し) means *to steam,* so note that these words are built from the root word *mushi.*

· *Asamushi* (浅蒸し) "shallow steam" or "light steamed" refers to a quick, usually 20–40 second steaming
· *Chumushi* (中蒸し) "medium steam" refers to a 40–80 second steaming
· *Futsumushi* (普通蒸し) "normal steam": the steaming time varies for each producer
· *Fukamushi* (深蒸し) "deep steam" refers to a longer steaming, usually 80 seconds or more

In order to steam the leaves, they are run through a mushiki (蒸機) or *steaming machine.* Steaming times can vary based on the ambient humidity at the time of steaming and the thickness of leaves used. Thicker leaves require a longer steam time to achieve the same results achieved by lightly steaming thinner leaves; think of the terms above as more of a continuum from shallow (asamushi) to deep (fukamushi) rather than a representation of exact steaming times.

Once steamed, rolled and dried, the tea leaves are called aracha (荒茶) or *crude tea*. Aracha is made up of unrefined, semi-processed tea leaves; it is sometimes called *farmers tea*. Aracha is produced by the farmer and then handed off to a factory for further sorting and processing. During the sorting process, any by-products created are called *demonocha* or *by-product tea*, a category that includes kukicha (stems), konacha (dust, fannings) and mecha (buds). While Japan may be famous for producing steamed teas, the Japanese are also well known for their much smaller production of kamairicha, a pan fired green tea, as well as several black teas. The majority of tea plants in Japan, 77% actually, are from the cultivar *Camellia sinensis* var. *sinensis* 'Yabukita'.[2]

Bancha dry leaves (5.7g) and liquor.

Bancha
(番茶)

The term *bancha* has many different regional meanings. In general it has become a term used to describe a lower grade steamed green tea style made from large leaves harvested any time after the first harvest (which is reserved for higher grade teas) or from larger leaves from early harvests. They are named either after the region in which they are produced or after variations in their processing steps. There are many different styles of bancha produced throughout Japan; translations of the word include *coarse tea*, *regional tea*, and *common tea*.

Sencha
(煎茶)

Steamed Tea

Sencha is arguably the most famous style of Japanese green tea. Fresh leaves are steamed, rolled, and dried, resulting in dark green needle-shaped finished tea leaves. Variations in the steaming time are used to produce several variants of sencha. In order of length of steaming time, the variants are asamushi (light steam), chumushi (medium steam), futsumushi (normal steam) and fukamushi (deep steam). The steaming time often varies, so one tea maker's fukamushi may resemble another's chumushi. In general, the longer the steaming process, the less pristine the final leaves will be as the steaming process breaks down the leaf structure.

Sencha dry leaves (11.7g) and liquor.

Kabusecha
(かぶせ茶)
Covered Tea *or* Shaded Tea
Kabusecha is a variant of sencha that is shaded for 1–2 weeks before harvest. This shading of the tea plants increases the concentration of amino acids and decreases the concentration of polyphenols in the leaves. The result is a less astringent tea with a stronger umami taste. This tea is sometimes spelled kabusesencha and its taste is often described as being between sencha and gyokuro.

Kabusecha dry
leaves (9.8g)
and liquor.

Gyokuro
(玉露)
Jade Dew

Gyokuro is produced in the same fashion as sencha; however the tea plants are shaded for three weeks before being harvested. This shading of the tea plants increases the concentration of amino acids and decreases the concentration of polyphenols in the leaves, resulting in a less astringent tea with a stronger umami taste.

Gyokuro dry leaves (11.3g) and liquor.

Shincha
(新茶)
New Tea

Shincha is a term used to denote the very first harvest of the season. These teas are typically processed like sencha but are steamed very lightly (asamushi) and dried less to show off their fresh properties. Because of the perishable nature of this very fresh tea, shincha is rushed to market once it is produced.

Shincha dry leaves (12.2g) and liquor.

Tencha
(碾茶)

Ground Tea

Tencha refers to tea leaves that are
ready to be made into matcha. Like
gyokuro, the tea plants used for making tencha are shaded for three weeks
before being harvested. Tencha starts
out as unrolled aracha that is then
sorted to remove the veins and stems.
The sorting process is usually done
using air, as veins and stems are heavi-
er than other leaf particles and can be
easily separated out. Tencha is made
up of flaky, dark green leaf bits.

Kamairicha
(釜炒り茶)
Tea Made in an Iron Pot

Aside from producing many styles of steamed green tea, Japan is also known for producing kamairicha, a pan-fired green tea. Kamairicha is pan-fired rather than steamed to halt oxidation, after which it is rolled and dried. Kamairicha is also considered a form of tamaryokucha because of its often curled shape.

Kamairicha dry leaves (9.7g) and liquor.

Tamaryokucha
(玉緑茶)
Curly Leaf Green Tea

Tamaryokucha means *curly leaf green tea* or *coiled green tea*. Fresh leaves destined to be tamaryokucha are steamed (mushi-sei, 蒸し製) or pan-fired (kamairi-sei, 釜炒り製), curled and dried resulting in curly dark green finished tea leaves.

Tamaryokucha dry leaves (10.2g) and liquor.

Temomicha
(手揉み茶)
Hand-Rolled Tea

Temomicha refers to hand-made green tea, often in the style of sencha. The leaves are hand-plucked and steam-fixed, and they are then rolled by hand into their distinctive needle-shape before being dried.

Temomicha dry leaves (10.9g) and liquor.

Demonocha
(出物茶)
By-Product Tea

Demonocha teas are made from stuff that has been sifted out, or stuff that has remained from making sencha, kabusecha and gyokuro. The three types of demonocha are kukicha (stems), konacha (dust, fannings) and mecha (buds).

Kukicha
(茎茶)
Twig Tea

Kukicha is made from the stems of sencha, kabusecha or gyokuro. Kukicha may also be called *bocha* or *stick tea*. Due to the fact that only the stems are used, this tea is naturally low in caffeine. When the stems are from gyokuro production, kukicha is often given the designation *karigane*.

Kukicha dry leaves (9.6g) and liquor.

Konacha
(粉茶)
Tea Powder

Konacha refers to the tiny fragments of tea leaves that are sorted out during the production of sencha, kabusecha and gyokuro. Even though konacha means tea powder, it isn't intentionally powdered. This sets it apart from truly powdered teas like matcha or funmatsucha. This is much like the *dust and fanning* grade of Indian teas, and it is often reserved for tea bags and served in sushi restaurants.

Konacha dry leaves (13.2g) and liquor.

Mecha
(芽茶)
Bud Tea

Mecha is made from the tiny buds that are removed from leaves destined for sencha, kabusecha or gyokuro during production.

Mecha dry leaves (13.4g) and liquor.

GREEN TEAS OF CHINA

The diversity of offerings that China gives us when it comes to green tea is vast. Nearly 74% of tea grown in China is green tea.[3] Some of the most famous teas that China produces are green teas, namely Xi Hu Long Jing and Dong Ting Bi Luo Chun.

Green Teas of Zhejiang Province

Anji Bai Cha
(安吉白茶, *ān jí bái chá*)
Anji White Tea

Anji Bai Cha is a style of green tea from Anji County in Zhejiang Province. The reason it bears the name *Anji White Tea* even though it is a green tea is due to the cultivar, *Camellia sinensis* var. *sinensis* 'Bai Ye 1'. The unprocessed tea leaves are whiter than they are green; the color of the liquor has been described as *white jade*. Thus the *bai cha* moniker is appropriate. Anji Bai Cha's finished leaves are yellow-green and needle shaped in appearance and expand once steeped to reveal their white color. To make this tea, fresh leaves are withered, pan-fired, shaped and then dried.

Anji Bai Cha dry leaves
(3.3g) and liquor.

Ping Shui Zhu
Cha dry leaves
(11.7g) and
liquor.

Ping Shui Zhu Cha
(平水 珠茶, *píng shuǐ zhū chá*)
Ping Shui Pearl Tea
This style of tea is produced in the
Ping Shui region of Zhejiang province. Famously known as *gunpowder
green tea*, Ping Shui Zhu Cha is made
up of leaves that have been withered,
steamed, and rolled into small pellets.
The pellets (or pearls) are dark green
and shiny. The pellets are sometimes
sprayed with rice paste to produce
their characteristic shiny sheen.[4]
Smaller pellets are associated with
high quality and fetch a higher price
than larger pellets.

Xi Hu Long Jing
(西湖 龙井, *xī hú lóng jǐng*)
West Lake Dragon Well

Long Jing is arguably the most famous style of Chinese green tea, and it also appears in the list of ten famous Chinese teas (see Appendix). Authentic Long Jing is grown in the areas surrounding West Lake in Zhejiang province's capital, Hangzhou. There are several cultivars being used for Long Jing, 'Changye', 'Qunti' and 'Long Jing #43' being the most prevalent. To make Long Jing, one bud and two leaves are plucked. The leaves are withered in the sun and then finished (fixed, shaped, dried) entirely in the pan. The finished leaves are pale green and flat.

Xi Hu Long Jing dry leaves (4.9g) and liquor.

Huang Shan
Mao Feng dry
leaves (2.8g)
and liquor.

Green Teas of Anhui Province

Huang Shan Mao Feng
(黄山毛峰, *huáng shān máo fēng*)
Yellow Mountain Fur Peak

This style of tea from Huang Shan in Anhui Province is one of China's ten famous teas. Maofeng means fur peak, but it also refers to the plucking standard (two leaves and a bud) of this tea and other teas that bear the Mao Feng name. This tea is produced by withering, fixing by forced air, and then rolling and drying fresh leaves. The finished tea leaves are slightly curled, yellow-green and very delicate; the plucking standard is usually left quite intact.

Lu An Gua Pian
(六安瓜片, *lù ān guā piān*)

Lu An Melon Seed

This style of tea produced in Anhui Province's Lu An County is one of China's ten famous teas. This tea is often made from older tea leaves whose shape resembles a melon seed. The leaves are withered, pan-fired, shaped and dried. The finished tea is made up of long, dark green leaves that have curled upon themselves longways toward the center.

Lu An Gua Pian
dry leaves (3.9g)
and liquor.

Tai Ping Hou Kui
(太平猴魁, *tài píng hóu kuí*)
Tai Ping Monkey King

This style of tea is traditionally grown in three villages in Anhui Province's Tai Ping County: Hou Keng, Hou Gan, and Yan Jia.[5] It is also one of China's ten famous teas. It is often made from a single bud and two large leaves from the 'Shi-da' cultivar that are withered, pan-fired, pressed between screens and then baked. The finished tea is made up of long pale green, very long flat-pressed leaves with a checkerboard pattern from the pressing that appear fleshy once brewed.

Tai Ping Hou Kui
dry leaves and
liquor.

Green Teas of Sichuan Province

Meng Ding Gan Lu
(蒙顶 甘露, *méng dǐng gān lòu*)
Misty Peak Sweet Dew
This style of tea is from the Meng Ding mountain area in Sichuan Province's Mingshan County. It is made up of mostly buds that are withered, pan-fired, rolled and then dried. The finished tea is very tippy; teas that contain a large percentage of buds are often given this label.

Meng Ding Gan Lu dry leaves (5.4g) and liquor.

Zhu Ye Qing
(竹叶青, *zhú yè qīng*)
Bamboo Leaf Green
This style of tea is from the Emei mountain area of Sichuan province. It is made up of single buds that are withered, pan-fired and dried. Zhu Ye Qing is a registered trademark of the Zhu Ye Qing Company, but many other farmers are producing this tea style in Sichuan.[6]

Zhu Ye Qing dry leaves (9.7g) and liquor.

Other Chinese Green Teas

Lu Shan Yun Wu
(庐山云雾, *lú shān yún wù*)
Lu Shan Clouds and Mist
This style of tea is from Lu Shan in Jiangxi Province. The name refers to the mountains shrouded in clouds and mist where this tea is grown. The finished tea is made up of leaves that are picked individually, withered, pan-fired, rolled into uniform dark green curls and dried.

Lu Shan Yun
Wu dry leaves
(7.2g) and liquor.

Dong Ting Bi Luo Chun
(洞庭 碧螺春, *dòng tíng bì luó chūn*)
Dong Ting Green Snail Spring

This style of tea is grown in the Dong Ting region in Jiangsu Province. Traditionally, Bi Luo Chun tea plants were planted together with fruit trees; this was done both for shade and in hopes that some of their flavor and fragrance would be imparted unto the Bi Luo Chun plants.

To make Bi Luo Chun, the bud and first leaf is plucked from the tea plant and withered. After withering, there are three processing steps: kill-green, shaping, and drying. All three processes are completed by hand in an iron pan or wok. The finished tea is made up of rolled tiny hairy green bud-sets that resemble green coiled snails. Dong Ting Bi Luo Chun is one of China's ten famous teas.

Dong Ting Bi Luo Chun dry leaves (5.9g) and liquor.

En Shi Yu Lu
(恩施玉露, *ēn shī yù lù*)
En Shi Jade Dew
This tea is produced in En Shi in Hubei Province. You may notice that this tea has the same translation as Japan's gyokuro, Jade Dew. To make this tea, one bud and one leaf or one bud and two leaves are harvested, withered, steamed, shaped and dried. Like gyokuro, the finished tea is made up of short dark green leaves.

En Shi Yu Lu
dry leaves (7.4g)
and liquor.

Xin Yang Mao Jian
(信阳 毛尖, *xìn yáng máo jiān*)

Xin Yang Fur Tip

Xin Yang Mao Jian is one of China's ten famous teas (see appendix). Mao Jian means *fur tip* but it also refers to the plucking standard (one leaf and a bud) of this tea and other teas that bear the Mao Jian name. The fresh leaves are withered, pan-fired, rolled and dried. The finished tea is made up of needle-shaped dark green leaves with furry tips (hence the name). This tea is produced in Xin Yang in Henan Province.

Xin Yang Mao Jian dry leaves (6.6g) and liquor.

South Korean Nok-Cha dry leaves (8.5g) and liquor.

GREEN TEAS OF KOREA

South Korea is home to three major green tea or nok-cha (녹차) producing regions: Boseong, Jiri Mountain, and Jeju Island. South Korean green tea is also known as bul-balhyocha (불 발효차) which means *not oxidized tea*. South Koreans produce both steamed green tea, jeung-cha (증차) and pan-fired green tea, bu-cha (부차). At times, small batches of jeung-cha are made by plunging the leaves into boiling water for fixing. Nearly all South Korean green teas are dried on a heated floor called a eundol (온돌). Green tea production in South Korea closely follows dates on the lunisolar calendar (see Chapter 2) and is often referred to as jakseol-cha 작설차 or sparrow's tongue tea.

chapter 7

Yellow Tea

Yellow tea is defined by a unique processing step where small batches of tea leaves are wrapped in cloth bundles after fixing, allowing them to yellow. The Mandarin term for this is *men huang* (闷黄, mēn huáng), which translates to *sealed yellowing*. While wrapped, the leaves turn from green to yellow-green as chlorophylls are broken down. Vegetal flavors mellow and subside, and the tea leaves partially oxidize.[1]

China is currently the only major producer of yellow
tea, and even there it is one of the less common types.
Yellow teas are not usually rolled or shaped in any way;
the original plucking standard is preserved.

Jun Shan Yin Zhen
(君山银针, *jūn shān yín zhēn*)
Junshan Silver Needle
This style of tea originated on Junshan
Island in Hunan Province's Dong
Ting Lake.[2] Junshan silver needle
is made up purely of buds that are
fixed, wrapped in small bundles and
dried. This tea is one of China's top ten
famous teas (see appendix); in fact, it is
the only yellow tea to make that list.

Jun Shan Yin Zhen dry
leaves (4.9g) and liquor.

Huang Ya
(霍山黄芽, *huáng yá*)
Yellow Sprout

Huang Ya is a name given to three famous yellow tea styles: Huoshan Huang Ya (霍山黄芽, *huò shān huáng yá*) originating in the Huoshan county area of Anhui province, Meng Ding Huang Ya (蒙顶黄芽, *méng dǐng huáng yá*) originating in the Meng Ding Shan area in Sichuan province, and Mo Gan Huang Ya (莫干黄芽, *mò gān huáng yá*) originating in the Mo Gan Shan area in Zhejiang province.

Huoshan Huang Ya is the easiest to find in the west, but what is sold is not always a yellow tea. Because the men huang process is difficult, laborious, and expensive, many producers are now skipping this part of the process. As this part of the process is the defining characteristic of yellow tea, these producers are actually selling green tea. Leaves destined to be Huoshan Huang Ya are pan-fired, wrapped in small bundles (or not), then dried. Meng Ding Huang Ya is typically made from buds only. Mo Gan Huang Ya is the hardest to find in the west.

Huoshan Huang Ya dry leaves (5.2g) and liquor. Meng Ding Huang Ya leaves (6.7) and liquor.

chapter 8

White Tea

White tea is made by withering fresh leaves for several days and then drying them. Another option is to wither the fresh leaves until they are dry. During this long wither, the leaves oxidize[1] slightly and aroma and flavor volatiles develop, giving white tea a more fragrant aroma than green or yellow tea.

The style of a white tea depends on any variations in this process. It also depends upon the cultivar of *Camellia sinensis* used, what combination of leaves and buds are picked, and the plant's terroir. These things are responsible for the many styles of white tea available to us on the market today. White teas are not rolled or shaped, so the structure of the fresh leaves remain intact in finished white tea. Despite being often described as such, white tea is not rare and white tea is not the most expensive tea. It is also not always made from just the buds of *Camellia sinensis*.

WITHERING AND DRYING

White tea leaves are subject to a long wither, and that extended wither provides the floral aromas that white teas are known for. To prolong the withering phase of white tea production, leaves are often withered in the shade first and then moved into the sun for final drying. If it is raining or too humid, the process will need to be adjusted. Essentially, almost all white teas are withered until they are dried, thus wearing out the enzyme activity responsible for oxidation.

WHITE TEAS OF CHINA

China's Fujian province is the home of white tea. It is most closely associated with the counties of Fuding and Zhenghe. The styles first created in Fujian are now being reproduced nearly everywhere tea is being grown.

Bai Hao Yin Zhen
(白毫银针, *bái háo yín zhēn*)
White Hair Silver Needle

This tea style is defined by the tiny tricomes (hairs) on the buds that give this tea a silvery white appearance. This tea originated in Fujian province in the counties of Fuding and Zhenghe. It is traditionally made from two regional cultivars of *Camellia sinensis* var. *sinensis:* 'Da Bai' (大白, *dà bái*) literally *large white* or 'Xiao Bai' (小白, *xiǎo bái*) literally *small white*. These cultivars are known for producing buds and leaves with a healthy coating of white tricomes. This tea is known for its sweetness as the bud of the tea plant contains energy in the form of sugar required to open up into a full budset. The buds also contain more caffeine than any other portion of the tea plant, mainly for protection against insects. It takes about 10,000 buds to make one kilogram of Bai Hao Yin Zhen.[2] To make this tea, buds are withered in the shade for several days and then moved into the sun to dry if the weather permits. Otherwise they are oven baked until dry.

Bai Hao Yin Zhen dry leaves (5g) and liquor.

Bai Mu Dan
(白牡丹, *bái mǔ dan*)
White Peony

Bai Mu Dan is a style of white tea that is made from the bud and one or two leaves of the Da Bai (大白, *dà bái*) literally *large white*, cultivar of *Camellia sinensis* var. *sinensis*. This tea is judged by the presence of *three whites*, meaning one white hairy bud and two leaves with white hairy undersides. To make bai mu dan, leaves are withered for several days and then baked to dry.

Bai Mu Dan dry leaves
(1.9g) and liquor.

Gong Mei
(贡眉, *gòng méi*)
Tribute Eyebrow

This style of tea follows the same processing methods used to make Bai Mu Dan. However, the finished tea is of lower quality; it often contains older leaves, broken leaves, and a smaller proportion of tips. The finished tea leaves are different shades of grey and green with a small proportion of tips.

Gong Mei dry leaves
(1.6g) and liquor.

Shou Mei
(寿眉, *shòu méi*)
Longevity Eyebrow

This style of tea follows the same processing methods used to make Bai Mu Dan and Gongmei. The finished tea is of lower quality than both of those styles; it often contains older leaves, broken leaves, and a smaller proportion of tips if any. Shou Mei is the most produced Chinese white tea style, accounting for more than 50% of total white tea production.[3]

Shou Mei dry leaves (2.0g) and liquor.

Yue Guang Bai dry leaves (2.8g) and liquor.

Yue Guang Bai
(月光白, *yuè guāng bái*)
Moonlight White

Yue Guang Bai is a style of white tea made from large leaf cultivars of the *Camellia sinensis* var. *assamica* plant. During processing the leaves are withered in darkness to prolong the withering time: hence the name *Moonlight White*. This withering process results in a complex, slightly oxidized and very aromatic tea. This tea originated in Yunnan province's Simao region. The finished tea is a mixture of buds and leaves, much like Bai Mu Dan; the major difference in appearance is that the leaves are nearly black on one side and covered with white hairs on the other.

Darjeeling Silver Tips

There are two notable white teas coming out of Darjeeling, India these days. One is *Silver Tips* from Okayti Estate, from the *Camellia sinensis* var. *sinensis* 'AV2' and *Camellia sinensis* var. *sinensis* 'P312' cultivars. The buds are harvested, withered for six to eight hours and then dried. Glenburn Estate is also producing a Silver Tips white tea. Glenburn's Silver Tips are produced from the buds of the *Camellia sinensis* var. *sinensis* 'AV2' cultivar. The buds are withered for 12–48 hours and then dried.

Glenburn Silver Tips dry leaves (4.0g) and liquor.

Sri Lanka Silver Tips

A notable white tea from Sri Lanka, Silver Tips hails from the gardens of PMD Tea in the Dimbula region. The cultivar in use there is *Camellia sinensis* var. *sinensis* 'TRI 2043.' The buds are withered, then dried.

PMD Dimbula Silver Tips dry leaves (4.2g) and liquor.

chapter 9

Wulong Tea

The word Wulong translates to *black dragon*. The proper pinyin is wūlóng (乌龙), but *oolong* (a haphazard transliteration) has become the most popular spelling in the West. This pronunciation is unlikely to die out, but the correct transliteration, wulong, is consistent with the romanization throughout this book.

Wulong leaves are semi-oxidized. This means that during production, oxidation is initiated, controlled and halted at some point before the leaves are considered fully oxidized. This is why you will often hear wulong described as being *in between* green tea and black tea. However, as with many things in the world of tea, it is more complicated than this.

A distinct step in the processing of traditional wulong tea is the bruising step (also called rattling or shaking). The leaves are shaken, lightly rolled or tumbled until the edges bruise. This bruising causes cellular damage and initiates the oxidation process. Bruising as a processing step is an iterative process wherein the leaves are bruised and allowed to wither and oxidize slowly.

The process happens repeatedly until they have reached a desired level of oxidation. The leaves are then heated (fixed) to stop oxidation and are shaped and dried.

Let's take a look at each step in a little more detail, beginning with the harvest.

PLUCKING

When plucking leaves for wulong production, tea pickers wait until the buds on the tea plant have opened and thickened. Depending on the intended shape of the final product, pickers will pluck anywhere from three to five leaves at a time. The reason for plucking older, thicker leaves is that they are more likely to endure the intense kneading and shaping required by the wulong production process.

WITHERING

Wulongs are typically withered in the sun or in diffused light under movable shades outdoors. Once the leaves are bruised, the withering process continues, often indoors. The withering process varies from producer to producer, but the goals of withering are the same: to prepare the leaves for further processing by making them flaccid. The withered leaves allow fragrance to develop.

BRUISING / OXIDATION

The distinct processing step that makes a wulong a wulong is bruising. The goal of bruising the leaves is to initiate oxidation. To do so, depending on the type of tea being made and the person making it, the leaves will be tumbled, shaken, or even lightly rolled (as is the case for many new non-traditional wulongs). When the leaves are bruised, the cell walls within the bruised portion of the leaves are broken, initiating oxidation. The leaves are then left to wither and oxidize before being further bruised. This iterative process continues until the desired level of oxidation is reached by the tea maker. Wulongs are often referred to as *semi-oxidized* teas and as such can be made at a wide range of oxidation levels. The greenest wulongs are oxidized to around 5–10%, while darker style wulongs are almost oxidized to black tea levels, around 80–90%.

FIXING

Once the desired level of oxidation is reached by repeatedly bruising the leaves and allowing them to wither, they are heated to prevent any further oxidation. Most wulongs are fixed by hot air in heated tumblers.

SHAPING

Traditionally, wulongs are processed into two different shapes: *half-ball shape* (also commonly referred to as partial-ball shape) and *strip shape* (also commonly referred to as stripe shape). Half-ball style wulongs are shaped using an iterative process called *cloth-wrapped kneading* where tea leaves are wrapped in cloth and kneaded. When this is done, the leaves clump together and form a tight ball. The leaf-mass is gently broken apart and then kneaded in cloth again. This process can go on for hours.

In most commercial applications, cloth-wrapped kneading is accomplished by a machine. However, small-scale artisan tea producers still knead the tea by hand (or even with their feet). Strip shaped wulongs are rolled by hand or by a machine without the use of cloth. They are twisted length-wise rather than rolled into a ball. During rolling, the amount of pressure exerted on the leaves is carefully monitored so that the leaves are not ripped apart.

Presentation of the finished tea is important to the tea producer, and a tea with a large percentage of stems is assumed to be a tea of lesser quality. Stems are picked off of finished tea leaves by hand or by machine before being packed and shipped. Sometimes stems are left on the finished leaves when sold. After all, this is a very laborious process, and tea is sold by weight.

Wulong stems from Fuzhou (3.4g).

DRYING AND ROASTING

Regardless of the shape of the leaves, once they are rolled or kneaded the mass of leaves is broken apart so that the leaves can be easily dried. In commercial production settings, wulong is dried in large ovens powered by electricity or gas. Smaller artisan production lines will use baskets over hot coals to slowly dry the leaves. This is often called firing or the first drying. Wulongs will often go through a second drying, also known as roasting. Roasting is done to mellow the tea's flavor and add to its complexity. At times, errors in processing can be hidden by a strong roasting step.

WULONG TEAS OF CHINA

About 11% of tea grown in China is wulong tea.[1] The majority of Chinese wulong production comes from the mountainous regions of Fujian Province. Fujian is home to the Anxi Tie Guan Yin and Wu Yi Yan Cha styles. The mountains of Wu Yi are the birthplace of wulong production, and the teas from that region are a testament to wulong's heritage.

Minnan Wulongs

Minnan wulongs refer to those produced *South of the Min [River]* in Fujian province. A famous growing region lies there, Anxi county. Anxi county is known primarily for the production of Tie Guan Yin, Huang Jin Gui, Ben Shan, Mao Xie, and the hybrid Jin Guan Yin. Anxi wulongs are difficult to tell apart by appearance alone, as they are usually produced in a similar half-ball style shape. Each one can be produced with varying levels of oxidation and roast. Oxidation and roast levels are altered slightly for each tea to preserve the qualities distinct to each cultivar and harvest. In general they are all processed in the same manner:

· withered in the sun
· tumbled to bruise the edges of the leaves
· withered (then bruised again, sometimes 20–30 times)
· fixed
· kneaded while wrapped in cloth (many times)
· dried[2]

Finished Anxi wulongs are almost always made up of single leaves that were broken off the stem by hand after drying.

Anxi Tie Guan Yin
(安溪 铁观音, *ān xī tiě guān yīn*)
Anxi Iron Goddess of Mercy

This tea style is produced in Fujian Province's Anxi county and is arguably the most famous wulong. Tie Guan Yin is made from the leaves of a cultivar with the same name, 'Tie Guan Yin.' Traditional versions of this tea are heavily roasted, but it is most commonly found in a green, unroasted state today. Tie Guan Yin is one of China's top ten famous teas; it is known for its floral fragrance and *hou yun* (喉韵) meaning *throat resonance* or *aftertaste*.

Light Anxi Tie Guan Yin dry leaves (8.7g) and liquor. Dark Anxi Tie Guan Yin dry leaves (10.8g) and liquor.

Anxi Huang Jin Gui
(安溪 黄金桂, *ān xī huáng jīn guì*)

Anxi Golden Cassia *or* Golden Osmanthus

This tea style is produced in Fujian Province's Anxi county and is very similar to Tie Guan Yin in appearance except for its yellow color. The yellowish color of the leaves is a characteristic of the 'Huang Jin Gui' cultivar. Huang Jin Gui is the earliest to flush of all the Anxi cultivars.

Anxi Huang Jin Gui dry leaves (10.4g) and liquor.

Anxi Ben Shan
(安溪 本山, *ān xī běn shān*)

Anxi Original Mountain

This tea style is produced in Fujian Province's Anxi county. Ben Shan is also very similar in appearance to Tie Guan Yin, the main difference being the cultivar this tea is made from, 'Ben Shan.'

Anxi Ben Shan dry leaves (9.2g) and liquor.

Anxi Mao Xie
(安溪 毛蟹, *ān xī máo xiè*)
Anxi Hairy Crab

This style of tea is produced in Fujian Province's Anxi county. Mao Xie is very similar in appearance to Tie Guan Yin, the distinguishing feature being the large amount of hairs on the leaves. The cultivar this tea is made from, 'Mao Xie,' is known to have hairy *crab-like* leaves.

Anxi Mao Xie dry leaves (10g) and liquor.

Anxi Jin Guan Yin
(安溪 金观音, *ān xī jīn guān yīn*)
Anxi Jin Guan Yin

Jin Guan Yin is a hybrid cultivar made from Tie Guan Yin and Huang Jin Gui. It is also a popular cultivar for the production of Wu Yi Yan Cha.

Anxi Jin Guan Yin dry leaves (9.3g) and liquor.

Minbei Wulongs

Minbei, or *North of Min [River]* refers to wulongs growing north of the Min river in Fujian province. The Wu Yi Yan Chas fall into this region. Yan Cha (岩茶, *yán chá*) means *rock tea;* it is a name given to the teas of Wu Yi Shan because the tea plants there are known to thrive in the rocky soils of the area. This unique terroir is responsible for the "rock taste" that gives these teas their fame. Known as Yan Yun (岩韵, *yán yùn*) literally *rock rhyme*, this is a way of describing the distinctive aftertaste yan cha is famous for.

All of the gardens in the Wu Yi area were propagated from four to six "mother trees" that still exist today and are a spectacle in the protected area of Wu Yi Shan. The further away from the protected Wu Yi area the plants are growing, the less sought after teas made from them are. There is actually a widely accepted nomenclature for this:

· Zheng Yan (正岩, *zhēng yán*), literally *center rock teas*, are grown inside the Wu Yi protected area.
· Ban Yan (半岩, *bàn yán*), literally *half rock teas*, are grown near the edges of the protected area.
· Zhou Cha (洲茶, *zhōu chá*) or *river bank teas* are grown well outside of the protected Wu Yi area.[3]

All Wu Yi teas are produced in nearly the same fashion. They are withered, tumbled, oxidized, fixed, rolled, dried and roasted. Wu Yi teas are formed into their distinctive strip shape by rolling the leaves length-wise on a rolling table.

Four Famous Wu Yi Teas

These teas are made from plants that have been propagated from the four famous bushes of Wu Yi Shan. They are often called Si Da Ming Cong (四大名丛) teas, meaning *Four Great Bushes*.

Wu Yi Da Hong Pao
(武夷 大红袍, *wǔ yí dà hóng páo*)
Wu Yi Big Red Robe

This style of tea is one of the two wulongs (Tie Guan Yin is the other) that make it to the list of top ten famous Chinese teas (see appendix). Big Red Robe is the most famous and widely produced of the Si Da Ming Cong teas. There is no specific Da Hong Pao cultivar; either Qi Dan (奇丹) or Bei Dou (北斗) are used or a blend is made from many different cultivars with the goal of creating a tea that best exemplifies Yan Yun (岩韵) or *rock rhyme*, the distinctive aftertaste of Wu Yi Yan Chas.

Wu Yi Da Hong Pao dry leaves (4.1g) and liquor.

Wu Yi Shui Jin Gui
(武夷 水金龟, *wǔ yí shuǐ jīn guī*)
Wu Yi Golden Water Turtle
This style of tea is a Wu Yi Si Da Ming Cong tea made from the 'Shui Jin Gui' cultivar.

Wu Yi Shui Jin Gui dry leaves (3.7g) and liquor.

Wu Yi Tie Luo Han
(武夷 铁罗漢, *wǔ yí tiě luó hàn*)
Wu Yi Iron Monk Arhat
This style of tea is the oldest of the Wu Yi Si Da Ming Cong tea made from the 'Tie Luo Han' cultivar.

Wu Yi Tie Luo Han dry leaves (4.6g) and liquor.

Wu Yi Bai Ji Guan
(武夷 白鸡冠, *wǔ yí bái jī guān*)

Wu Yi White Cockscomb

This is known in China as a Wu Yi Si Da Ming Cong style of tea. The leaves from the 'Bai Ji Guan' cultivar appear white-ish, hence the name. The finished tea is made up of long, curled yellow-brown strips.

Wu Yi Bai Ji Guan dry leaves (4.5g) and liquor.

Other Wu Yi Cultivars
These cultivars are not included in the Si Da Ming Cong (四大名丛) teas and are sometimes called Qi Zhong (奇种)—literally, *the weird kinds.*

Wu Yi Rou Gui
(武夷 肉桂, *wǔ yí ròu guì*)
Wu Yi Cassia *or* Wu Yi Cinnamon
This style of Wu Yi tea is named after the distinctive cinnamon notes in tea steeped from teas made from the 'Ro Gui' cultivar.

Wu Yi Rou Gui dry leaves (4.6g) and liquor.

Wu Yi Shui Xian
(武夷 水仙, *wǔ yí shuǐ xiān*)
Wu Yi Narcissus
This style of Wu Yi tea is known for notes of honey in the tea liquor made from its leaves. The 'Shui Xian' cultivar is often grown elsewhere outside of the Wu Yi area, but it is usually still processed like a Wu Yi wulong.

Wu Yi Shui Xian dry leaves (3.8g) and liquor.

Wulongs of Guangdong Province

Feng Huang Dan Cong
(凤凰单丛, *fèng huáng dān cōng*)

Feng Huang single bush or single trunk Dan Cong refers to a style of strip-shaped wulong production wherein leaves are plucked and processed from single trees. The original plants were propagated by seed over 700 years ago in the Phoenix Mountain (Feng Huang Shan) region. They have been harvested and processed individually since, hence the name Dan Cong or *single bush*. The tea producers noticed that each plant produced tea that tasted different. Dan Cong teas are a perfect example of selective breeding, as the plants were named after the fragrance of the finished teas they produced and have since been asexually cloned for commercial production.

Feng Huang Dan Cong dry leaves (3.5g) and liquor.

Authentic Dan Cong teas must be grown within the Phoenix Mountain area in Guangdong's Chao An County and must come from one of the famous cultivars. It is thought that all of the Dan Cong cultivars are descendants of the 'Shui Xian' cultivar. Here are some of the well-known cultivars (note that xiang '香' means *fragrance*):

Gui Hua Xiang
(桂花香, *guì huā xiāng*)
Osmanthus Fragrance

Huang Zhi Xiang
(黄栀香, *huáng zhī xiāng*)
Gardenia Fragrance

Jiang Hua Xiang
(姜花香, *jiāng huā xiāng*)
Ginger Flower Fragrance

Mi Lan Xiang
(米蘭香, *mǐ lán xiāng*)
Honey Orchid Fragrance

Rou Gui Xiang
(肉桂香, *ròu guì xiāng*)
Cinnamon Fragrance

Xing Ren Xiang
(杏仁香, *xìng rén xiāng*)
Almond Fragrance

Ya Shi Xiang
(鸭屎香, *yā shǐ xiāng*)
Duck Shit Fragrance

You Hua Xiang
(柚花香, *yòu huā xiāng*)
Pomelo Flower Fragrance

Yu Lan Xiang
(玉兰香, *yù lán xiāng*)
Magnolia Flower Fragrance

Zhi Lan Xiang
(芝蘭香, *zhī lán xiāng*)
Orchid Fragrance

Other Chinese Wulongs

Lan Gui Ren
(兰贵人, *lán guì rén*)
Lady Orchid
This tea is also known as Ginseng
Wulong because the tea is processed
with powdered American Ginseng
root and licorice root powder and then
rolled into tiny solid-looking pellets.

Lan Gui Ren dry leaves
(13.9g) and liquor.

WULONGS OF TAIWAN

Formerly known as Formosa, Taiwan is a small island that lies on the Tropic of Cancer just off the east coast of Fujian province. Taiwan occupies an area just 0.4% the size of mainland China. Given its proximity to Fujian province, Taiwan is famous for its production of wulong tea; 90% of tea produced there is wulong.[4] The island is able to produce a myriad of wulong styles due to the micro-climates of the different growing regions, a product of the vast differences in elevation across the island. Because Pinyin only became the standard method of romanization in Taiwan in 2009, you will likely encounter many Wade-Giles spellings of tea terms when purchasing Taiwan wulongs.

Nantou Dong Ding
(南投 冻顶, *nán tóu dòng dǐng*)
Nantou Frozen Summit

Arguably the most famous of the half-ball-style Taiwan wulongs hails from Nantou County in central Taiwan from the areas surrounding Dong Ding mountain. Dong Ding wulong is typically produced using leaves from the 'Qing Xin' cultivar of tea plant. Fresh leaves destined to become Dong Ding wulong are withered in the sun and tumbled to bruise the edges of the leaves. Next an iterative process begins wherein the leaves are withered, then bruised further many times. Once the desired amount of oxidation has been reached, the leaves are fixed. Once fixed, the leaves are kneaded while wrapped in cloth. The leaf mass forms a tight ball that is then carefully broken apart and kneaded again. This step is responsible for forming the half-ball shape of these wulongs. Once the desired shape is achieved, the leaves are dried. Dong Ding wulongs are typically produced with lower amounts of roast and oxidation.

Nantou Dong Ding dry leaves (13.2g) and liquor.

**Muzha Tie Guan Yin
(木栅 铁观音, *mù zhà tiě guān yīn*)**
Muzha Iron Goddess of Mercy
Muzha Tie Guan Yin is Taiwan's version of Fujian's half-ball style Tie Guan Yin. Traditionally, this tea was heavily roasted before being sold, but today the trend seems to be that wulongs sell better when roasted very little, or not at all. Muzha Tie Guan Yin is a half ball-style wulong produced from the 'Tie Guan Yin' cultivar using the cloth-wrapped kneading process.

Muzha Tie
Guan Yin dry
leaves (12.8g)
and liquor.

Wen Shan Bao Zhong
(文山 包种, *wén shān bāo zhǒng*)
Wen Shan Wrapped Kind

Bao Zhong is a strip-style wulong from the Wen Shan area of Northern Taiwan. Compared to other Taiwan wulongs, Bao Zhong is typically the least oxidized wulong style. Its oxidation levels are usually well under 20%. The name "wrapped kind" comes from an old packaging method where Bao Zhong leaves were packaged in folded paper wrapping for selling. To make Bao Zhong, leaves from the 'Qing Xin' cultivar are withered in the sun, withered indoors, lightly tossed to initiate oxidation, rolled and dried.

Wen Shan Bao Zhong dry leaves (3.8g) and liquor.

Dong Fang Mei Ren dry leaves (5.6g) and liquor.

Dong Fang Mei Ren
(东方美人, *dōng fāng měi rén*)

Oriental Beauty

This style of tea is also known as *Bai Hao* or *White Tip* wulong due to the use of buds in the finished tea. Dong Fang Mei Ren hails from the Hsinchu City area of Northern Taiwan and is produced from the 'Qing Xin Da Mao' cultivar. This strip-shaped wulong is heavily withered and heavily oxidized to 70–80%. The oxidation process starts while the leaves are still attached to the plant in the field once the unsprayed leaves are bitten by jassids and other insects. The plant in turn creates more polyphenols to inhibit further insect attack.

Gao Shan
(高山, *gāo shān*)
High Mountain

Literally *High Mountain*, Gao Shan is a designation given to any wulong grown at an elevation higher than 1000m. The most famous growing regions above 1000m are Ali Shan, Shan Lin Xi, Li Shan and Da Yu Ling. Da Yu Ling is the highest growing mountain at 2400m. Teas grown in these regions are usually less oxidized and unroasted in order to show off the special qualities that these high mountain teas possess. Qing Xin, Jin Xuan, Cuiyu and Si Ji Chun are the most popular cultivars of tea plant cultivated in the high mountain regions.

Gao Shan (Jin Xuan from Alishan) dry leaves (13.9g) and liquor.

Famous Taiwan Wulong Cultivars
These cultivars are sometimes sold by name only; other times they are grown above 1000m and called Gao Shan. The reason I list them out here is that you will often see them called out by name.

Jin Xuan dry leaves (13.6g) and liquor.

Jin Xuan
(金萱, *jīn xuān*)
Golden Lily

Jin Xuan is a famous cultivar from Taiwan known for producing a creamy mouthfeel and milk-like aroma or *nai xiang* (奶香) when steeped. Many "milk wulongs" on the market will contain artificial flavorings, but true Jin Xuan possesses nai xiang without any adulterants. This cultivar was created by the Tea Research and Extension Station and is also known as TRES #12.

Si Ji Chun
(四季春, *sì jì chūn*)
Four Seasons of Spring
As its name suggests, this cultivar produces a fragrant spring-like crop year round. Because of this, it has also been given the nickname *evergreen*.

Si Ji Chun dry leaves (12.6g) and liquor.

Cuiyu
(翠玉. *cuì yù*)
Green Jade
This cultivar is popular for making lightly oxidized or jade wulongs. This cultivar was created by the Tea Research and Extension Station and is also known as TRES #13.

Cuiyu dry leaves (12.7g) and liquor.

Qing Xin
(青心, *qīng xīn*)
Green Heart
This cultivar is also called *Ruan Zhi* (軟枝). Ruan Zhi means *soft stem*, and it is often transliterated as *Luan Ze*.

Qing Xin dry leaves (14.5g) and liquor.

Other Tawanese Teas

Gui Fei
(贵妃, *guì fēi*)
Precious Concubine
Gui Fei is a style of tea that is processed
similarly to Dong Feng Meiren except
that it is rolled into a half-ball shape
instead of strip shape. Just like Dong
Feng Mei Ren, it is grown pesticide-free
and is allowed to be bitten by jassids.
Gui Fei is often highly oxidized and
lightly roasted.

Gui Fei dry
leaves (12.6g)
and liquor.

Jia Xie Long
Cha dry leaves
(10.7g) and
liquor.

Jia Xie Long Cha
(佳叶龙茶, *jiā xié lóng chá*)
GABA Tea

This style of tea is exposed to nitrogen during oxidation. The presence of nitrogen and absence of oxygen during processing converts glutamic acid to gamma-Aminobutyric acid, or GABA. GABA tea can really be produced as any type of oxidized tea, but it is most often produced as wulong. GABA has been touted for its health benefits for years, but recent research suggests that GABA is unable to cross the blood-brain barrier, thus discounting many of the health claims made by GABA producers.

OTHER WULONG TEAS

Nearly every tea producing region in the world has some small, experimental wulong production, though none are as famed as the wulongs from China and Taiwan.

Thailand Wulong

The area surrounding Chiang Mai and Chiang Rai is home to many tea gardens that produce wulong tea. The gardens mostly grow Taiwan tea cultivars and use Taiwan wulong processing methods and machinery to produce clones of famous Taiwan wulongs. While they are growing in popularity as Thai wulongs, many of the wulongs produced in this region are marketed as Taiwan wulongs. Tea production in Thailand was started by the Thai government as a *Royal Development Project* in order to curb the production of opium in the area. The most renowned production area is Doe Mae Salong.

Thai Wulong dry leaves (12.4g) and liquor.

chapter 10

Black Tea

Black teas are often described as fully oxidized teas. To be more accurate, let's say mostly oxidized. The basic process for making black tea from fresh tea leaves is withering, rolling, oxidation, and drying. The goal of black tea production is to induce and control oxidation until the tea leaves achieve a prescribed level of oxidation.

Black tea is the most produced tea type in the world. It is important to note that what most of the world outside of East Asia refers to as black tea is known to the Chinese (and most Asian countries) as *red tea* (红 茶, hong cha). Calling this tea type black tea is confusing because the Chinese already have a tea category called Hei Cha (黑茶) which translates to black/dark tea (see Chapter 11, Fermented Tea). Calling this tea type red tea is also confusing because most of the western world uses the term red tea for African Rooibos, which isn't tea at all but rather a tisane from leaves from the *Aspalathus linearis* bush. Sometimes when I'm feeling a tad snobby and referring specifically to Chinese teas, I'll call it red tea. I call this tea type *black tea* in the following chapter to avoid confusion.

PATH TO OXIDATION

After withering, leaves destined to be black tea undergo the most important step in their journey—the initiation of oxidation. This can take on several forms, but the goal is always the same: to break the cell walls within the leaves so that the polyphenols mix with the enzymes polyphenol oxidase and peroxidase, thus initiating oxidation. If it is commodity CTC (crush-tear-curl) tea we're making, the leaves are macerated using a rotorvane or a CTC machine. This quick and harsh destruction of the leaves results in a quick and harsh oxidation. If we're making whole-leaf teas, the leaves are rolled instead of destroyed. Rolling is usually done using an orthodox rolling table these days; the process is done less and less by hand. Rolling tables apply pressure while rolling the tea out. If enough pressure is applied, the leaves will break.[1]

Once oxidation is initiated, it is closely controlled by introducing warm, moist, oxygen-rich air over time. The length of oxidation depends on "the temperature, the degree of maceration, the degree of wither, and the type of tea to be produced."[2] The more polyphenols in the leaves, the more potential for flavor development during oxidation when the flavanols are converted into theaflavins and thearubigins. Once the tea leaves have reached their desired level of oxidation, they are dried. CTC teas are typically dried on endless-chain perforated conveyors or on a fluidized bed of hot air. Black teas can also be dried in an oven on perforated trays or outdoors in the sun. Drying halts the enzyme activity within the leaves and makes them shelf stable.

BLACK TEAS OF CHINA

Only 6% of finished tea produced in China is black tea,[3] but the quality and range of Chinese black tea has yet to be challenged by any other tea-producing nation.

Black Teas of Fujian Province

Often categorized as *Bohea*, a haphazard transliteration of the Northern Fujian *Wu Yi* mountains, these black teas include the famous Lapsang Souchong from Tong Mu village. Other notable Fujian province black teas are the smoked teas from the regions surrounding Tong Mu village, Golden Monkey, and three famous Gongfu teas.

Zheng Shan
Xiao Zhong
dry leaves (5.8g)
and liquor.

Zheng Shan Xiao Zhong
(正山小种, *zhēng shān xiǎo zhǒng*)

Mount Zheng Small Variety

Zheng Shan Xiao Zhong is often romanized as Lapsang Souchong.[4] It was probably the first black tea ever commercially produced. Originating in Fujian Province's Tong Mu Village in the Wu Yi Shan area, this tea style is processed in a 3–4 story smoking shed called a *qinglou* (清 楼). At the bottom of a qinglou is a wood oven where horsetail pine is burned, producing smoke throughout the levels of the shed. The tea leaves are withered on the top levels, oxidized on the middle levels and dried in the bottom levels. The withering and oxidation process of this tea takes place in the qinglou, imparting the smoke aroma on the leaves. The finished tea is strip shaped and solid black with a characteristic smoky aroma and notes of longan fruit. You may find that some merchants call all black teas from the Wu Yi Shan area Lapsang Souchong whether traditionally smoked or not.

Yan Xiao Zhong
(烟小种, *yān xiǎo zhǒng*)
Smoked Small Kind

Yan Xiao Zhong is a style of tea that is smoke dried, or smoked after being dried. Sometimes called *smoked souchongs*, these refer to those smoked teas other than Tong Mu village's Lapsang Souchong. The finished tea is strip shaped and solid black with a characteristic smoky aroma.

Yan Xiao Zhong dry leaves (7.9g) and liquor.

Jin Jun Mei
(金骏眉, *jīn jùn méi*)
Golden Steed Eyebrow

Jin Jun Mei is a high grade tea style from Tong Mu village made solely of buds. The use of buds alone gives the tea its distinct golden sheen. This tea is produced from the Wu Yi Cai Cha group of cultivars, and it is withered, rolled, allowed to oxidize, and dried. As the name suggests, the finished tea is made up of strips of golden brown leaves.

Jin Jun Mei dry leaves (5g) and liquor.

Jin Hou Hong Cha
(金猴红茶, *jīn hóu hóng chá*)
Golden Monkey Red Tea
This tea style is produced in many varying grades dependent upon the percentage of golden tips that make up the finished tea. This tea was once produced throughout Fujian province; however, its production has been largely replaced by variants of the more marketable Jin Jun Mei.

Jin Hou Hong Cha dry leaves (6.6g) and liquor.

Bailin Gongfu
(白琳工夫, *bái lín gōng fū*)
This tea is arguably the most famous of Fujian province's three famous gong-fu style teas. Produced in Bailin village in Fuding County from the 'Da Bai' or *big white cultivar*, this tea is withered, rolled, oxidized and then bake dried. The finished tea is strip shaped, long and wiry with black and fuzzy gold leaves.

Bailin Gongfu dry leaves (7g) and liquor.

Zhenghe Gongfu
(政和 工夫, *zhèng hé gōng fū*)
This tea is one of the three famous
Gongfu teas from Fujian province.
Produced in Zhenghe county from the
'Da Bai' or *big white cultivar*, this tea
is withered, rolled, oxidized and then
bake dried. The finished tea is strip-
shaped, long and wiry with black and
gold leaves.

Zhenghe Gongfu dry
leaves (6.4g) and liquor.

Tanyang Gongfu
(坦洋工夫, *tǎn yáng gōng fū*)
This tea is one of the three famous
Gongfu teas from Fujian province.
Produced in Tanyang Village from the
'TanYang Cai Cha' group of cultivars,
this tea is withered, rolled, oxidized
and then bake dried. The finished tea
is strip shaped, long and wiry with
black and gold leaves.

Tanyang Gongfu dry
leaves (6.1g) and liquor.

Black Teas of Yunnan Province

Black teas from Yunnan Province are collectively referred to as Dian Hong (滇红, *diān hóng*), literally *Yunnan Red*. This term originally referred only to black teas from Feng Qing County, but it is increasingly being applied to any black tea produced in Yunnan province. There are many styles of Dian Hong on the market today ranging from CTC to full leaf tea. Dian Hongs do have one thing in common; they are all made from the 'Feng Qing Daye Cha' cultivar, a descendant of the *assamica* variety of *Camellia sinensis*.

Dian Hong Gongfu
(滇紅工夫, *diān hóng gōng fū*)

Yunnan Red Gongfu

Dian Hong Gongfu is a tea style that is produced in many variants. Some differ by the plucking standard used in production, and some exhibit elaborate shapes. These teas are often marketed as *Yunnan Gold* in the west because the budsets used to produce these teas turn gold once oxidized.

Diang Hong Gongfu dry leaves (8.5g) and liquor.

Dian Hong Jin Ya
(滇紅金芽. *diān hóng jīn yá*)
Yunnan Red Golden Shoot

Dian Hong Jin Ya is a black tea made solely of golden buds produced in China's Yunnan province. The oxidized buds turn gold, hence the name "golden shoot." There are several variations of this tea on the market; two common variants are Jin Zhen (金针) or *Golden Needle* and Jin Si (金丝) or *Golden Threads*.

Dian Hong Jin Ya dry leaves (4.7g) and liquor.

Black Teas of Anhui

Anhui province is home to perhaps the most famous Chinese black tea, Qimen (祁门, qí mén). Qimen is often spelled "Keemun," a haphazard transliteration whose usage has become quite common in the tea industry. Qimen is named after Anhui province's Qimen county and is produced in several styles. The styles Hao Ya, Mao Feng and Xin Ya are collectively known as Qi Hong (祁红), short for Qimen Red. These teas are from the 'Zhu Ye Zhong' (楮叶种) cultivar and are all withered, rolled, oxidized, and dried. Qimen is one of China's top ten famous teas (see Appendix), and it is the only black tea to make it to the list.

Qimen Hao Ya
(祁門毫芽, *qí mén háo yá*)
Qimen Downy Sprout

Qimen Hao Ya is the most common representation of Qi Hong tea. It comes in two grades, Hao Ya A and Hao Ya B. The A grade has more tips than the B grade variant. This tea is produced much like the orthodox teas of India, as it is rolled on a rolling table which breaks it into small uniform pieces. The finished tea is made up of small pieces of leaves and buds about 1cm in length.

Qimen Hao Ya A dry
leaves (12.9g) and liquor.

Qimen Mao Feng
(祁門毛峰, *qí mén máo fēng*)

Qimen Downy Tip

Qimen Mao Feng is made by hand with slightly twisted full leaves, often two leaves and a bud. The finished tea leaves are black with golden tips.

Qimen Mao Feng dry leaves (6.2g) and liquor.

Rie Yue Tan
Hong Cha
dry leaves (4.1g)
and liquor.

BLACK TEAS OF TAIWAN

Ri Yue Tan Hong Cha
(日月潭紅茶, *rì yuè tán hóng chá*)
Sun Moon Lake Red Tea

Ri Yue Tan is a style of black tea grown in the Sun Moon Lake area of Taiwan's Nantou County. Sun Moon Lake typically refers to black tea made from cultivars of the *assamica* variety of *Camellia sinensis* which was planted throughout the Sun Moon Lake area by the Japanese during their occupation of Taiwan.

Hong Yu
(紅玉, *hóng yù*)
Red Jade

This refers to Taiwan black teas created from a hybrid of a native Taiwan variety and a Burmese variety of tea plant. The tea is characterized by menthol notes, and it was produced by the Taiwan Tea Research and Extension Station. The official Taiwan Tea Research and Extension Station name for this cultivar is 'TRES #18,' and tea made from it often bears the name *Ruby #18* in the West.

Hong Yu
dry leaves (4.6g)
and liquor.

BLACK TEAS OF INDIA

The Indian tea industry at large is focused on the production of commodity black tea. In fact, 85% of tea produced in India is CTC black tea.[5] Tea is produced in the Southern regions of Munnar in Kerala and Nilgiri in Tamil Nadu and the Northern regions of Darjeeling in West Bengal, Assam in Assam, and Kangra in Himachal Pradesh. The two main tea producing areas are Darjeeling and Assam.

There are two methods of initiating oxidation employed in Indian tea manufacture: the orthodox method by rolling, and the CTC (Crush Tear Curl) method of crushing, tearing, and curling the leaves. Virtually all tea producing regions in India employ one or both of these production methods. The orthodox process is used when making specialty tea. The orthodox process employs a rolling table unless the leaves are rolled by hand. The rolling table uses a combination of rotation and pressure to roll the leaves, twisting them and breaking them into pieces. It is the sorting process done after drying that gives us a uniform leaf particle size, as well as the many grades of Indian tea.

Darjeeling Black Tea

The Darjeeling region in India's West Bengal state is home to 87 registered tea gardens ranging from 600–2000m in elevation. These gardens produce several distinct products based on the different flushes or growth period of the tea plants.

First Flush Darjeeling teas are typically rolled to a lesser degree and less oxidized (typically to about 35%) than other flushes to preserve the fresh nature of the leaves. Because of their semi-oxidized nature, many tea aficionados consider First Flush Darjeeling teas wulongs. Second Flush Darjeeling teas are more akin to black teas; they begin with fresh tea leaves and are withered, rolled, oxidized, dried and sorted. The leaves are broken during the rolling process and after being dried are sorted into many grades based on particle size. This is why, though broken, the leaf particles from finished Darjeeling teas are of uniform size. Darjeeling's terroir is famous for producing a muscatel flavor in the teas produced there.

First Flush Darjeeling (Goomtee) dry leaves (7.5g) and liquor. Second Flush Darjeeling (Castleton) dry leaves (5.7g) and liquor.

List of 87 Registered Tea Gardens of Darjeeling

Alloobari
Ambiok (Hillton)
Ambootia
Arya
Avongrove
Badamtam
Balasun
Bannockburn
Barnesbeg
Castleton
Chamong
Chongtong (Siristi)
Dhajea
Dilaram
Dooteriah
Edenvale
Giddapahar
Gielle
Ging
Glenburn
Goomtee
Gopaldhara
Gyabaree & Millikthong
Happy Valley
Jogamaya
Jungpana (Jungpana Upper)
Kalej Valley
Kanchan View
Kumai (Snowview)
Lingia

Liza Hill
Longview (Highlands)
Lopchu
Mahalderam
Makaibari
Margaret's Hope
Marybong
Mim
Mission Hill
Mohan Majhua
Monteviot
Moondakotee
Mullootar
Nagri
Nagri Farm
Namring & Namring (Upper)
Narbada Majhua
North Tukvar
Nurbong
Oaks
Okayti
Orange Valley (Bloomfield)
Pandam
Pashok
Phoobsering
Phuguri
Poobong
Pussimbing (Minzoo)
Rangaroon
Ringtong

Risheehat
Rohini
Runglee Rungliot
Rungmook/Cedars
Samabeong
Seeyok (Spring Valley)
Selim Hill
Selimbong (Rongbong)
Sepoydhoorah (Chamling)
Singbulli
Singell
Singtom
Sivitar
Soom

Soureni
Springside
Steinthal
Sungma
Teesta Valley
Thurbo
Tindharia
Tukdah
Tukvar (Puttabong)
Tumsong
Turzum
Upper Fagu
Vah Tukvar Sri Dwarika T.E.

Assam CTC dry leaves (11.1g) and liquor.

Assam Black Tea

The Assam region is the largest tea production region in India both by size and by amount of tea produced. There are around 800 tea estates in Assam, most of them at or around sea level. Nearly all of the tea plants grown in Assam are *Camellia sinensis* var. *assamica*. There are two methods of initiating oxidation employed in Indian tea manufacture: the orthodox method by rolling and the CTC (Crush Tear Curl) method of crushing, tearing, and curling the leaves. Assam primarily uses the CTC method wherein the leaves are withered, macerated using a rotorvane or a CTC machine, allowed to oxidize, dried then sorted. Finished teas from Assam are notably dark, brisk and malty. They are primarily produced for blending into breakfast teas, masala blends, and other blends that are typically taken with the addition of milk.

BLACK TEAS OF KENYA

Kenya is the world's third largest tea producer. The country almost solely produces CTC (Crush Tear Curl) black tea from *assamica* clones. CTC is a processing method used to produce homogenous commodity tea wherein tea leaves are macerated during production. Most Kenyan tea is grown in highland regions between 1500 and 2700 meters high where temperatures are lower and rainfall is greater. Production in Kenya goes on year-round, with two peak production seasons that coincide with rainy seasons in March and June and October and December.

Kenya (Milima GFBOP1) dry leaves (7.3g) and liquor.

A Note about Kenyan Purple Tea

The Tea Research Foundation of Kenya (TRFK) has produced an *assamica* cultivar rich in anthocyanin called TRFK 306 with a purple appearance. Several growers in Kenya are purporting to have created a new type of tea from a classification sense, "Purple Tea." It is important to note however that this is not a new type of tea; the leaves are harvested like any other cultivar and are processed into either green or black tea. Remember, tea types are defined by processing methods, not cultivar. It is also important to note that cultivars rich in anthocyanin have been cultivated in China, Sri Lanka and India for many years.

Sri Lanka Black
(Lumbini FBOP)
dry leaves (7.2g)
and liquor.

BLACK TEAS OF SRI LANKA

Sri Lanka (also called *Ceylon* from the days of British occupation) is the world's 4th largest tea producer. Orthodox black tea accounts for 95% of the country's total tea production.[6]

Sri Lankan tea is categorized by region and elevation. The main production regions are Nuwara Eliya, Dimbula, Kandy, Uda Pussellawa, Uva, and Ruhuna. Elevation of production ranges from near sea level to 1800m above sea level. Tea grown below 600m is designated *low country*, tea grown between 600 and 1200m is called *mid country*, and tea grown above 1200m is called *up country* or *high country*. Tea is harvested year-round in Sri Lanka, mainly from hybrids of var. *assamica* and var. *sinensis* plants. Finished tea produced in Dimbula and Uva during their dry seasons is world renowned for its exquisite flavor and aroma.[7]

BLACK TEAS OF JAPAN

Wakoucha (和紅茶) or *Japan Red Tea* refers to black teas that are produced in Japan. While the overwhelming majority of tea produced in Japan is green tea, there has been some experimentation with black tea. Black tea cultivars (mostly Assam hybrids) have been around since before the 1950s. Registered black tea cultivars in Japan include:

Japan Black dry leaves (6.9g) and liquor.

Benihomare
Indo
Hatsumomiji
Benitachiwase
Akane
Benikaori
Benifuji
Satsumabeni
Benihikari
Benifuki

Note that *beni* is a Japanese word for *red.*

chapter 11

Fermented Tea

The fermented tea category is perhaps the least understood tea category in the West. This category encompasses a wide array of finished tea styles that differ in processing, raw materials, shapes and sizes. Fermented teas do all share one common processing activity: intentional fermentation.

Fermentation in tea refers to the breakdown of substances by bacteria, yeasts or other microorganisms. It is usually initiated using one or a combination of the following methods:

1. Indigenous microorganisms already present in the raw material initiate it
2. A small amount of fermented tea leaves are added to unfermented tea leaves
3. Starter cultures are added to the raw material
4. Indigenous microorganisms in the area where the fermentation occurs initiates it

FERMENTED TEAS OF CHINA

China is by far the largest producer of fermented teas in the world, yet only 3% of tea produced in China falls into the fermented tea category.[1] Hunan, Anhui, Sichuan, Guangxi and Hubei are known for the production of a variety of fermented teas called hei cha (黑茶, *hēi chá*) or *dark* tea.

Yunnan is known for its famous *Puer* tea which is produced in two ways. *Sheng Puer* is a tea that is allowed to naturally ferment and oxidize over time, and *Shu Puer* is pile-fermented, a process utilized to mimic the results of the slow maturation found in *Sheng Puer*.

Fermentation vs. Oxidation

It is worth mentioning that the word fermentation has a rather confusing history in the world of tea. True fermentation refers to the breakdown of substances by bacteria, yeasts or other microorganisms, but for many years it was thought that the darkening of tea leaves during processing was a result of fermentation rather than oxidation. Some tea producing countries still refer to oxidized teas as having gone through fermentation. To make matters more confusing, during true fermentation polyphenols in tea leaves are actually oxidized by enzymes derived from the microorganisms appearing in the fermentation process. So when we're talking tea processing, finished teas that are oxidized are not fermented but finished teas that are fermented have gone through some oxidation.

Whether or not Puer falls under the hei cha category is a long-held point of contention among tea drinkers; I'll point out the differences below.

Nearly all Chinese fermented teas (Sheng Puer being the major exception) share a processing step called wo dui (渥堆, *wò dūi*) which means *wet piling*. During wo dui, tea leaves are put into piles and moisture is added and controlled over a period of several hours to several weeks depending on the type of fermented tea being manufactured. The piles are covered and the leaves are turned over from time to time during the process.

Let's take a look at the diverse world of Chinese fermented teas, beginning with hei cha.

Hunan Hei Cha

Most hei cha comes from Hunan Province, where Anhua County is the center of Hunan hei cha production. The people of Hunan province first produced hei cha 1400 years ago in the Tang Dynasty.

Hei Mao Cha
(黑猫茶, *hēi māo chá*)
Semi-Finished Dark Tea

Nearly all styles of Hunan hei cha begin with the production of Hei Mao Cha or *semi-finished dark tea*. Hei Mao Cha is made by fixing, rolling, pile-fermenting and drying fresh tea leaves, usually from descendants of *Camellia sinensis* var. *assamica* known as Da Ye Zhong (大叶种) or *large leaf type*. Another way to refer to Hei Mao Cha is *pile-fermented Mao Cha.*

Hei Zhuan Cha
(黑砖茶, *hēi zhuān chá*)
Dark Brick *or* Black Brick Tea
Hei Zhuan Cha is a fermented tea made by steaming Hei Mao Cha and pressing it into special rectangular molds. The bricks are then dried in a warm room and wrapped. The finished product is a rectangular brick with a flat surface, usually without markings.

2011 Hei Zhuan Cha
(1kg, 24×13×3.5cm) and
liquor.

Fu Zhuan Cha
(茯砖茶, *fú zhuān chá*)
Fu Brick Tea

Fu Zhuan Cha is a style of fermented tea made by steaming Hei Mao Cha and pressing it into special rectangular molds or bricks. The bricks are then wrapped in paper and dried very slowly in a warm room. The size and weight of Fu Bricks may vary. These bricks are known for the presence of *jin hua* (金花) or *golden flowers* throughout the bricks. These golden flowers are actually a beneficial mold known as *Eurotium cristatum* that is known in the world of Chinese medicine for having many health benefits. The production of this style of Hei Cha has expanded beyond Hunan Province in recent years.

Fu Zhuan Cha (500g, 20×10×3cm) and liquor.

Hua Zhuan Cha
(花砖茶, *huā zhuān chá*)

Flower Brick Tea

Hua Zhuan Cha is a style of rectangular Hei Cha brick with ornate designs on the surface. Hua Zhuan cha is made by steaming Hei Mao Cha and pressing it into special rectangular molds. In order for the designs on the bricks to be well defined, the pressing is much harder for flower bricks and the resulting bricks are much tighter than other bricks. The bricks are then dried in a warm room and wrapped in paper.

2012 Hua Zhuan Cha
(1kg, 23.5×14×3cm) and
liquor.

Hua Juan Cha
(花卷茶, *huā juǎn chá*)
Flower Roll Tea

Hua Juan refers to a style of cylindrical Hunan hei cha. This tea is produced in several variants that are named after the weight of the finished tea. The Hei Mao Cha used for Hua Juan Cha typically comes from the 'Yuntai Shan' (云台山) cultivar of *Camellia sinensis* var. *assamica*. Hua Juan Cha is produced by pounding steamed Hei Mao Cha into a cylindrical bamboo basket lined with a layer of bamboo leaves and a layer of palm husk. The cylinder is then pounded with a large wooden hammer as it is rolled tight by several people. It is then tied off and allowed to dry outdoors for several weeks.

Each Hua Juan variant uses a Chinese weight measure called a tael (两.). During the Qing dynasty when this style of tea was first produced, a Tael was equal to 36.25g. The most common sizes produced are Qian Liang Cha (千两茶, *qiān liǎng chá*) or *thousand tael tea*, Bai Liang Cha (百两茶, *bǎi liǎng chá*) or *hundred tael tea* and Shi Liang Cha (十两茶, *shí liǎng chá*) or *ten tael tea*.

HUA JUAN VARIANTS

NAME	TRANSLATION	WEIGHT	HEIGHT	DIAMETER
Qian Liang Cha	thousand tael tea	36.25kg	150–160cm	20cm
Bai Liang Cha	hundred tael tea	3.625kg	60–65cm	10cm
Shi Liang Cha	ten tael tea	362.5kg	20–25cm	5cm

Qian Liang Cha: wrapped slice, unwrapped slice and liquor.

Bai Liang Cha slice
and liquor.

Bamboo-wrapped
Shi Liang Cha
and liquor.

Xiang Jian Cha
(湘尖茶, *xiāng jiān chá*)
Hunan Tip Tea

Xiang Jian Cha refers to a style of loose hei cha made in Hunan Province. Xiang Jian Cha is made by fixing, rolling, pile-fermenting, rolling, and drying fresh tea leaves. The loose tea is broken up into three different grades. In descending order of quality they are Tian Jian (天尖茶) or *heaven tips*, Gong Jian (贡尖茶) or *tribute tips* and Sheng Jian (生尖茶) or *raw tips*. These teas are sold loosely-packed into baskets of varying sizes.

Xiang Jian Cha basket (1kg, 13cm wide, 24cm long, 15cm high), dry leaves and liquor.

Qu Jiang Bao Pian Cha
(渠江薄片茶, *qú jiāng báo piàn chá*)
Qu Jiang Thin Slice Tea

Qu Jiang Bao Pian Cha was the first style of hei cha ever produced. This tea was first produced during the Tang Dynasty near Qu Jiang town in Hunan's Anhua County. This tea is made by compressing steamed and ground Hei Mao Cha into coin shapes, thus the name "thin slice".

Qu Jiang Bao Pian Cha
(4cm diameter, 4mm
thick) and liquor.

Sichuan Hei Cha

Notorious for hei cha loaded with stems and twigs as well as older tea leaves, Sichuan Heicha is often called *Tibetan Tea* or *border tea*. This tea style can be separated into two groups named after where it was sold historically, Nan Lu Bian Cha (南路边茶, *nán lù biān chá*) or *South Border Tea*, and Xi Lu Bian Cha (西路边茶, *xī lù biān chá*) or *West Border Tea*. Nan Lu Bian Cha can be further broken into Kang Zhuan and Jin Jian Cha. Xi Lu Bian Cha can be further broken into Fu Zhuan, which was first made in Sichuan though most production has moved to Hunan after the Sichuan farmers could not meet demand, and Fangbao Cha.

Kang Zhuan Cha
(康砖茶, *kāng zhuān*)
Peaceful Brick

Kang Zhuan is a style of Nan Lu Bian
Hei Cha brick from Sichuan province.
Kang Zhuan is made up of a mixture
of older tea leaves and stems. The stem
content must be less than 8% of the
total brick. Leaves and stems destined
for Kang Zhuan are fixed, rolled, and
pile-fermented. Once fermentation is
complete, they are pressed into rectangular bricks with a distinct pillow
shape on one end from the mold. The
bricks are then dried and wrapped
in their signature yellow paper. Kang
Zhuan tea is the tea of choice when
making Tibetan Yak Butter Tea.
Production of this tea has spread from
Sichuan to Hunan and Guizhou.

Kang Zhuan Cha
(500g, 17×10×3.5cm)
and liquor.

Jin Jian Cha
(12.6g) and
liquor.

Jin Jian Cha
(金尖茶, *jīn jiān chá*)
Golden Tip Tea

Jin Jian tea is a style of Sichuan Nan
Lu Bian Hei Cha produced in the
same manner as Kang Zhuan. It is also
pressed into a rectangular brick shape.
Leaves and stems destined for Jin Jian
Cha are fixed, rolled and pile-fermented. Once fermentation is complete,
they are pressed into rectangular
bricks. The major difference between
Jin Jian and Kang Zhuan is quality;
Jin Jian is produced with lower quality materials. Quality is maintained by
the rule that stem content must be less
than 15% of the total brick.

Fang Bao Cha
(方包茶, *fāng bāo chá*)
Square Wrapped Tea

Fang Bao Cha refers to a style of Sichuan Xi Lu Bian Heicha. Leaves and stems destined to become Fang Bao Cha are fixed, rolled, and pile-fermented. Once fermentation is complete, the leaves are pressed into large square bricks and are wrapped in woven bamboo. Fang Bao Cha is often also wrapped in animal skins. Each finished brick weighs about 35kg, and one can be strapped to each side of a horse for transportation.

Fang Bao Cha
(11.4g) and
liquor.

Anhui Hei Cha

Lu An Hei Cha
(六安黑茶, *lù ān hēi chá*)
Lu An Dark Tea

Lu An Hei Cha production began in the areas surrounding Lu An city in Anhui Province. Lu An Hei Cha is made from small tea leaves that are fixed, rolled, pile-fermented and dried. The resulting leaves are then sorted, blended, steamed and packed into woven bamboo baskets lined with bamboo leaves. Basket size will vary with most common baskets weighing 500g. The baskets are often wrapped in stacks of six, and six stacks are put into a larger basket, making 36 total.

Lu An Hei Cha basket (500g, 16.5cm long, 10.5cm wide, 9cm tall), dry leaves and liquor.

Hubei Heicha

Qing Zhuan Cha
(青砖茶, *qīng zhuān chá*)
Green Brick Tea

Qing Zhuan is a style of hei cha brick from Hubei. This tea is also sometimes called Lao Qing Cha (老青茶) or *old green brick.* Qing Zhuan is largely made from old leaves and stems; sometimes these bricks are comprised of up to 25% stems. The bricks are made by withering, fixing, rolling and pile-fermenting fresh tea leaves and then pressing them into a brick shape with three distinct markings on the front.

Qing Zhuan (2kg,
15×33×4cm) and liquor.

Liu Bao Cha dry leaves (7.5g) and liquor.

Guangxi Heicha

Liu Bao Cha
(六堡茶, *liù bǎo chá*)
Liu Bao Tea

This style of hei cha is named after the town where it originated, Liu Bao in China's Guangxi Province. Liu Bao Hei Cha is made from tea leaves from *Camellia sinensis* var. *sinensis* that are fixed, rolled, and dried. The dry leaves are then pile-fermented, a process where the leaves are piled, moisture is added, and the leaves are covered and allowed to ferment. Once fermentation is complete, the leaves are sorted, blended, steamed and pressed into large woven bamboo baskets lined with bamboo leaves for aging. Finished Liu Bao baskets weigh between 20–60kg depending on the producer. Liu Bao is often packaged in smaller, 1kg baskets for individual selling.

Yunnan Puer

Puer 普洱 (pǔ ěr) is arguably the most famous fermented tea in China. Widespread speculation led to a meteoric rise in Puer popularity and price, with a tenfold increase in prices seen from 1999 to 2007. Overspeculation led to a bubble that burst in 2007. Puer prices still fluctuate, and some regional Puer teas still remain some of the most expensive teas in China.

To be considered a Puer, the tea leaves must be grown in Yunnan Province and must be from descendants of *Camellia sinensis* var. *assamica*, known colloquially as Da Ye Zhong (大叶种) or *large leaf type*. The leaves must also be dried in the sun.

There are two styles of Puer, Sheng Puer and Shu Puer. Each style begins with Puer Mao Cha (毛茶), literally *coarse tea* or *unfinished tea*. Puer Mao Cha, the raw material for Puer, is made by pan-firing large leaves from the Da Ye Zhong variety of *Camellia sinensis*, rolling the leaves, and then drying them in the sun. At this point, the Mao Cha can be made into Shu Puer or Sheng Puer; the only differences are the processing methods for each, which are explained below.

Historically Puer was compressed for easy transport, but today Puer tea leaves are compressed into shapes for three reasons: presentation, aging, and dosing.

Bing Cha (100g, 10cm diameter).

Fang Cha (100g, 8.25×8.25cm).

Here are the most popular Puer shapes:

Bing Cha
(饼茶, *bǐng chá*)
Cake Tea
Refers to tea leaves pressed into a round flat disk or cake shape.

Fang Cha
(方茶, *fāng chá*)
Square Tea
Refers to tea leaves pressed into squares.

Tuo Cha
(沱茶, *tuó chá*)
Bowl Shape Tea
Refers to tea leaves pressed into shapes that resemble a birds nest.

Jin Gua Cha
(金瓜茶, *jīn guā chá*)
Golden Melon Tea
Also known as melon-shaped tea, refers to tea leaves pressed into a melon-shape.

Jin Cha
(紧茶, *jǐn chá*)
Tight Tea
Refers to tea leaves formed into a mushroom shape.

Tuo Cha (100g, 7.5cm wide at opening, 5cm tall).

Jin Gua Cha (250g, 10cm wide at base, 6.5cm tall).

Jin Cha (250g, 10cm at widest portion, 9cm tall).

Ju Pu Cha
(29.5g, 5cm
diameter,
3.5cm tall).

Puer is also often pressed into items such as oranges (Ju Pu Cha: 菊普茶, *jú pǔ chá*), pomelos (You Zi Cha: 柚子茶, *yòu zi chá*) and bamboo culms (Zhu Tong Cha: 竹筒茶, *zhú tŏng chá*).

Bing Cha is the most common shape of compressed Puer tea on the market. Because bings commonly fetch steep prices, they are often counterfeited. Producers have taken several steps to help curb counterfeiting. First, a small label, basically a *certificate of authenticity* is literally compressed into the bing. This label is called a Nei Fei (内飞). Another label, called a Nei Piao (内票) is placed on top of the bing before it is wrapped in paper. The paper wrapping is printed with the name of the tea and the factory that produced it.

The most common weight for a bing is 357 grams. The reason for this seemingly odd number has to do with how tea was historically transported. Wrapped bings are stacked in piles of seven and are covered with a bamboo sheath. They are then wrapped with bamboo thread or wire. The package is called a *Tong* (筒, literally *tube*). 12 tongs are packed together into a larger woven bamboo basket called a *Jian* (件) weighing about 30kg. A mule can carry approximately 60kg, so one 30kg jian was strapped to either side of a mule for transport.

Puer Mao Cha
(普洱毛茶, *pǔ ěr máo chá*)
Puer Coarse (Unfinished) Tea

Puer Mao Cha is the base material used both for Sheng and Shu Puer production. Puer Mao Cha is produced by withering and then pan-firing large leaves from plants that are descendents of *Camellia sinensis* var. *assamica*, known colloquially as 'Da Ye Zhong' (大叶种) or *large leaf type*. After being fixed, the leaves are rolled and dried in the sun. It is important to note that the temperature of the fixing step is lower than that used for other teas; the lower temperature helps to retain some of the flavanols responsible for oxidation.

Puer Mao Cha
(3.2g) and
liquor.

Sheng Puer
Cha (100g,
10cm diameter)
and liquor.

Sheng Puer Cha
(生普洱茶, *shēng pǔ ěr chá*)
Raw Puer Tea

Literally *Raw Puer Tea*, Sheng Puer
is a style of Puer wherein Puer Mao
Cha is aged naturally over time. Aging
here refers to a combination of oxidation and fermentation. Sheng Puer
is sold loose or compressed into various shapes (most commonly bings).
The taste of Sheng Puer is enhanced
with proper aging, and older bings
that have been stored properly can be
worth large amounts of money. This
style of Puer is primarily responsible
for the Puer bubble of 2007.[2] Sheng
Puer made from the leaves of old trees,
known as Gushu (古树), is particularly
prized. Because this tea is also enjoyed
in a fresh unfermented state, there
is some debate in the tea world over
whether or not Sheng Puer should be
considered a fermented tea.

Shu Puer Cha
(熟普洱茶, *shú pǔ ěr chá*)

Ripened Puer Tea

Shu Puer is a style of Puer wherein Puer Mao Cha is *pile-fermented*, a process known as Wo Dui (渥堆) or *wet piling*. Wet piling was developed in 1973 to mimic the results of slow-aged Sheng Puer. During pile fermentation, Puer Mao Cha is piled and covered with damp cloths. Additional moisture is added to the pile, and the leaves are left to ferment for around 45 days, being turned occasionally to promote even fermentation. Once complete, the leaves are dried, sorted and either compressed or sold loose.

Shu Puer Cha (200g, 14cm diameter) and liquor.

JAPANESE FERMENTED TEA

There are a several interesting fermented teas produced in Japan, most being local variants of bancha. The most famous variants are goishicha, awabancha, and batabatacha.

Goishicha
(碁石茶)

Goishicha is variant of bancha wherein fresh tea leaves are steamed and then carefully stacked, packed and covered for fermentation. Once fermented, the packed leaves are cut into pieces and dried in the sun.

Goishicha (4.6g) and liquor.

Awabancha
(阿波番茶)

Awabancha is a variant of bancha wherein fresh tea leaves are first plunged into boiling water, halting the oxidation. The leaves are then rolled and pressed into barrels to ferment. Once the leaves are removed from the barrels, they are dried and packaged.

Awabancha dry leaves (1.8g) and liquor.

Bancha Batabatacha
(バタバタ茶)

Bancha Batabatacha is a variant of bancha wherein fresh tea leaves are pan fired until they begin to turn yellow and brown to halt oxidation. The leaves are then partially dried and placed into wooden boxes for fermentation. Once fermentation is complete, the leaves are dried in the sun.[3]

Bancha Batabatacha dry leaves (2.7g) and liquor.

chapter 12

Altered Tea

Altered teas refer to teas that go through additional processing steps during or after primary processing before being sold. This can refer to flavoring, scenting, blending, smoking, aging, decaffeinating or grinding. The majority of teas sold in the United States are altered in some way.

FLAVORED AND SCENTED TEA

Flavored and scented teas are a big business in the West; the market for them is much larger than the market for single-origin pure teas. The main reason is accessibility via familiarity. When flavoring or scenting, tea merchants are able to add a familiar flavor to a tea and market the tea only by its flavor. Ginger Peach and Earl Grey are examples of popular black tea flavors in the United States. You will seldom be told more than the type of tea that was flavored when purchasing a flavored or scented tea. Oftentimes, flavorings are added to cheap *base teas*, an industry term for cheap, usually broken leaf teas with a homogenous taste that take on flavors well. Flavors often mask the nuances imparted by terroir and cultivar, and flavoring would not make sense if done to more expensive specialty tea leaves.

Flavoring tea means adding flavors to already processed tea leaves via inclusions, extracts, or natural and artificial flavoring agents. Inclusions refer to additions such as spices, fruit pieces, or flower petals that are actually mixed in to be steeped with the tea. The amount of inclusions used for a specific tea varies widely based on the desired end result. Extracts and flavoring agents are typically infused into a solvent such as propylene glycol, glycerin, benzyl alcohol, ethyl alcohol, or triacetin and added to tea leaves. These solvents quickly evaporate after application, leaving the flavors behind on the tea.[1] Essential oils are also sometimes used to flavor teas. In this case, the oils are sprayed and mixed with tea leaves and allowed to dry before packaging. Once the flavoring process is complete, an extract, flavoring agent, or essential oil can make up anywhere from 0.5% to 5% of a flavored tea by weight.[2]

Scenting a tea is a slightly different process that takes advantage of the natural tendency of processed tea leaves to take on the scent of their surroundings. To scent a tea, tea leaves are simply left in close proximity to the aroma-providing ingredient. At times, heat and humidity may be used to aid in the scenting process. The aroma-providing ingredient is then removed, and the tea leaves retain that ingredient's aroma. Common scented teas are jasmine, osmanthus, rose, chrysanthemum and lotus blossom.

Earl Grey
Earl Grey tea is a style of black tea first created in England that is flavored or scented with the oils or zest from the flavedo of the bergamot orange (*Citrus bergamia*). Sometimes inclusions of bergamot rind or cornflower petals may be seen in Earl Grey. The base tea used for Earl Grey is typically a strong broken black tea from Assam or Sri Lanka.

Earl Grey dry leaves
(6.7g) and liquor.

Masala Chai dry leaves (12.9g) and liquor.

Masala Chai
(मसाला चाय)

Masala Chai is a style of black tea with spice inclusions. The word *chai* is a common transliteration of Hindi's *chāy*, meaning *tea*, and *masala* is derived from the Hindi word for *spice mix*. Therefore, *masala chai* translates to *spice mix tea*. Masala Chai is so popular in India that it is often shortened and just called *chai*. This has led to much of the Western world referring to Masala Chai as "Chai Tea" which means "Tea Tea."

The street version of masala chai is often blended on the street by a chai-wallah and decocted with water and milk. For the purposes of this chapter, I'm referring to the version of Masala Chai we're most likely to find in the West, a blend of broken Assam tea leaves mixed with any combination of spices. Typical spices found in masala chai are cardamom, cloves, cinnamon, ginger, black pepper, star anise, and nutmeg.

Japanese Genmaicha (玄米茶)

Genmaicha is an inclusion tea made by adding roasted white rice (roasted rice turns brown, hence the name) to Japanese green tea. Genmaicha can be made from any Japanese green tea, but it is typically made from bancha or sencha.

Japanese Genmaicha dry leaves (6.7g) and liquor.

Jasmine Pearls dry leaves (13.1g) and liquor.

Jasmine Tea
(茉莉花茶, *mò lì huā chá*)

Jasmine Tea most commonly refers to styles of Chinese green tea that have been scented with blossoms from the *Jasminum sambac* plant. Great care is taken to create jasmine-scented tea. Fresh jasmine blossoms are mixed in with green tea and a small amount of heat is applied to the mixture. The two ingredients intermingle for a few hours to a few days, and the blossoms are then sieved out and discarded. In more commercial applications, the blossoms are removed from the tea leaves using a vibrating platform. During higher quality jasmine tea production, this process will be repeated several times and the ratio of jasmine blossoms to tea will be much higher.

BLENDED TEA

Tea blending is a practice commonly adopted by tea companies who seek to produce a homogenous product year after year. Blending allows a tea merchant to maintain a signature taste; any changes in taste caused by weather or faulty processing can be hidden. This is a common practice in the production of commodity tea where consistency and cost-control are key to business. In fact, a single Lipton tea bag can contain tea leaves from up to 40 different finished teas. Blending may also be done to achieve a tea taste that is not possible with a single tea. Chinese Da Hong Pao wulong and Japanese greens such as sencha and matcha are often products of careful blending.

Breakfast Tea

Perhaps the best examples of blended tea are the many styles of breakfast teas. English Breakfast, Irish Breakfast, and Scottish Breakfast all are blended black teas. Teas that make up these blends are often from the countries of Kenya, Sri Lanka, Assam, China, and Indonesia. Breakfast tea recipes vary from company to company, but the end goal is the same among them—to produce a strong black tea that can stand up to the addition of cream and sugar.

English Breakfast dry leaves (10.5g) and liquor.

ROASTED TEA

As discussed in Chapter 4, roasting is a form of drying used to enhance flavor. Roasting is most common among the wulongs of China and Taiwan and in the production of Japanese Hojicha. Most roasting of tea leaves is done in an electric oven, but tea roasting was traditionally done on bamboo baskets over charcoal.

Roasted Wulong

Wulongs not only vary greatly in terms of the amount of oxidation that is allowed to occur in the leaves during processing, but wulongs also vary greatly by level of roast. Roasting here is a form of heat drying used to enhance flavor. Traditionally, roasting was achieved using bamboo baskets over hot charcoal. Today most roasting is done using electric ovens. Regardless of method, the idea is simple: the lower the temperature and the longer the roast, the higher quality the end result will be. Nearly all wulongs produced in China and Taiwan can be found on the market with varying levels of roast. During roasting, amino acids in the tea leaves are transformed into aromatic compounds by way of the Maillard reaction, resulting in a toasty, nutty flavor development in the tea.[3] Roasting is also a useful tool when aging wulongs, as it aids in reducing the moisture content in the leaves absorbed during aging.

Roasted Wulong (12g) and liquor.

Hojicha dry leaves (4.1g) and liquor.

Hojicha
(ほうじ茶)
Roasted Tea

Hojicha (also spelled houjicha) translates to *roasted tea*. Hojicha is a style of roasted Japanese green tea typically made by roasting bancha, sencha, or kukicha. The roasted tea leaves are varying degrees of brown depending on the length and intensity of the roasting process. Hojicha can be made at home by lightly roasting bancha, sencha or kukicha in a dry pan or by using a ceramic vessel known as a *Hojicha Iriki* over a small flame, keeping the temperature around 200 degrees Celcius.

AGED TEA

Any finished tea can be aged, but certain teas *mature* more gracefully than others. The tea types that you are most likely to see aged are fermented teas and wulong teas. Fermented teas are often aged in an environment that is not airtight; airflow, temperature, and humidity are monitored and adjusted over time to control the aging of the tea. In this case, aging refers to the slow fermentation and oxidation of tea leaves. In all other cases, aging is largely a very slow controlled oxidation of tea leaves, which is why you rarely see teas that are fully oxidized being aged. Wulongs are often stored in airtight vessels and are occasionally removed and re-roasted during aging. There is also a particular style of Japanese green tea production called Kuradashi that requires aging.

Kuradashi
Yabukita sencha
(10.5g) and
liquor.

Kuradashi
(蔵出し)

Literally *bring out of cellar*, Kuradashi is a style of Japanese green tea (usually gyokuro or matcha) that has been aged. Traditionally, tea leaves are stored in wooden boxes in a cool environment for several months to several years to mellow. When making Kuradashi matcha, the matcha itself is not aged. Instead, the tencha is aged and then ground into matcha before packaging up for shipping. This is because the increased surface area of matcha would cause the tea to deteriorate rather than age gracefully.

Aged Puer

Aging Puer typically refers to the slow fermentation and oxidation of Sheng Puer over time by controlling temperature, humidity and airflow. Too much humidity and too little airflow can result in a moldy tea. Puer storage is a very controversial topic; Puer collectors have deliberated over ideal storage conditions for many years with little consensus. Storage methods have been categorized by the level of relative humidity, from *natural storage* to *dry storage* to *wet storage*. Volumes have been written on this topic, so I won't cover it here. I will however, impart a few tidbits on how this all works.

The higher the level of humidity and the higher the temperature where Puer tea is stored, the faster fermentation and oxidation will occur. The lower the level of humidity and the lower the temperature where Puer tea is stored, the slower fermentation and oxidation will occur. Dry storage is at one end of the humidity continuum and wet storage is at the other. If done incorrectly, wet storage can result in a musty, sometimes fishy smelling tea.

DECAFFEINATED TEA

All teas made from *Camellia sinensis* contain caffeine; even those that have been decaffeinated retain a small portion of caffeine. Decaffeination is a process wherein a solvent is used to remove the caffeine from tea leaves. Methylene Chloride used to be the solvent of choice, but health concerns resulted in its use being banned in the United States. Today, Ethyl Acetate and Supercritical Carbon Dioxide are the commonly used solvents.

Ethyl Acetate was the first solvent to be used; it is not very effective in the removal of caffeine, and it also removes some of the flavor providing compounds within the leaves. Supercritical Carbon Dioxide is a better choice; it is able to remove caffeine without affecting any other compounds within the leaves. To decaffeinate tea leaves, the solvent is mixed with oxidized tea leaves. After several hours, the solvent and the dissolved caffeine is removed and the leaves are dried.[4]

GROUND TEA

The practice of grinding tea leaves predates loose leaf tea as we know it today. Japan still holds to the tradition of grinding tea leaves to produce two finished teas: Matcha and Funmatsucha.

Funmatsucha
(粉末茶)
Powdered Tea

Funmatsucha differs from matcha in that is it not made from tencha. In fact, any powdered tea not made from tencha is considered Funmatsucha. Funmatsucha is often made from sencha.

Funmatsucha powder (11.4g) and whisked funmatsucha.

Matcha powder (8.6g) and whisked matcha.

Matcha
(抹茶)
Fine Powder Tea

Matcha is a style of green tea made from tencha (often blended) that has been ground into a very fine powder. Matcha particles are typically 10–15 microns in size.[5] Matcha is a very bright green powder ground in a large granite mill called an *ishiusu*. Matcha is often produced in two grades: ceremonial grade and ingredient grade. The difference between the two grades will differ from company to company, but determining factors include whether the tencha was hand or machine picked, whether the tencha was ground by a hand-powered mill or by a machine-powered mill, and by the season of harvest.

The major difference between matcha and other teas (besides the fact that it is ground into a powder) is that it is typically prepared using a whisk to create a suspension of tea powder in hot water. In order for a powdered tea to be called matcha, it must be made from tencha; other ground teas are called *Funmatsucha*. For the language nerds, 抹茶 actually romanizes to maccha but is typically spelled matcha.

OUTLIERS

Cha Gao
(茶膏, *chá gāo*)
Tea Paste

Cha Gao is made from a reduction of decocted Shu Puer. The leaves are slowly boiled until the liquor is reduced to a paste; this can also be accomplished by spray drying the steeped tea. The resulting hard, shiny black substance is sold in many forms, and it is often seen pressed into decorative shapes. To prepare this tea, a small piece of Cha Gao is chipped off and dissolved in hot water.

Cha Gao (18g)
and liquor.

South Korean Hwang Cha dry leaves (4.5g) and liquor.

South Korean Hwang Cha (황차)

South Korean Yellow Tea

Hwang Cha is a tea that is made by withering, heaping and then drying tea leaves on a heated floor called a *eundol* (온돌). Because of the lack of a fixing step during processing, many refuse to consider Hwang Cha for the yellow tea category. This tea is also given the balhyocha (발효차) label, which means oxidized tea; the balhyocha label can be applied to any oxidized tea regardless of the level of oxidation. The lack of the fixing step results in a partially oxidized tea; in Korean, the term for this is bubun balhyocha (부분 발효차).

South Korean Tteok Cha (떡차)

South Korean Rice Cake Tea

One notable compressed tea that is not produced in China hails from South Korea. It is *Tteok Cha*. Tteok is the Korean term for *rice cake*. Similar to traditional rice cake production, steamed tea leaves are pounded into a pulpy mass, formed into coin shapes and strung together with string for drying and storing.[6] This tea is similar to China's Qu Jiang Bao Pian Hei Cha.

South Korean Tteok Cha and liquor.

Ya Bao (芽苞, *yá bāo*)

Sprouting Bud

Ya Bao refers to the unopened bud from wild tea plants of the Da Ye Zhong variety from China's Yunnan Province. These buds appear in late winter and early spring. Once harvested, they are either treated like a white tea and withered until dry or treated like a green tea and fixed before being dried.

Ya Bao (5.2g) and liquor.

enjoying tea

chapter 13

Kinetics of Steeping

You've arrived at the most important part of this book ... the entire reason for your tea journey. In this part you will learn how to enjoy tea. The chapters in this section cover everything involved with tea preparation, including tea evaluation and tea storage. We'll begin with tea preparation, known to many as *steeping*.

Steeping is the final step in the lives of tea leaves. And in their final act, they slowly unfold and unravel, creating a beverage that tells the story of where they came from. Every time we drink liquor from the steeped leaves, it tells us what the weather was like before they were plucked and how they were handled, processed, and stored before they reached your cup.

Chemically speaking, steeping refers to the act of infusing tea leaves in a *solvent* (water) to make a *solution* that is on average 98% water and 2% compounds from within the tea leaves.

But what actually happens during steeping? When tea leaves are added to water, they absorb some of it and become rehydrated. This absorption of water into the tea leaves allows for the initiation of steeping, the process of extracting the soluble compounds from the tea leaves and dissolving them in water. The driving force of the steeping process is the difference in concentrations of dissolved compounds in the leaves and the water. Compounds in the leaves move from an area of high concentration to an area of low concentration until equilibrium is achieved, a process called *diffusion*[1].

The type of tea being steeped is the most important determinant when it comes to the types and amounts of soluble compounds within tea leaves. Tea types are defined by the processing steps the leaves go through, and thus the resulting chemical components are similar for all styles of finished tea within a type. Across all tea types, the major chemical components in tea leaves fall into the following categories: polyphenols, amino acids, enzymes, pigments, carbohydrates, alkaloids, minerals and volatiles. Individual chemical components lend themselves to a portion of the cup in the form of taste, color or body. The chemical composition of a cup of tea depends not only on the chemical compounds found within the leaves, but also the chemical properties of the water, the surface area of the leaves, the ratio of leaves to water, steeping temperature, and the length of time the leaves are in contact with water.

chapter 14

Water Quality

Steeped tea is 98% water, which is why using a high quality water source for tea preparation is of utmost importance. But what does it mean for a water to be high quality, or *good* for tea? There are so many aphorisms that attempt to define how water should be prepared for tea—most of them, pardon my pun, *hold no water*. Common ones are: use freshly drawn cold water, don't re-boil water, don't overboil water, and use water with a high amount of dissolved oxygen. In my experience, these things will do little if anything at all to enhance your tea experience.

For a water source to be suitable for tea preparation we must be sure it tastes good on its own. But what does this mean? Let's examine the common properties of water, including mineral content, hardness, and pH level, and then discuss ways we can obtain water of ideal quality.

MINERAL CONTENT

Good tasting water has a balance of minerals and a clean, even taste. Too high of a mineral content will make water taste tinny and metallic—but a low mineral content will make water taste dull. Mineral content is often erroneously associated with total dissolved solids (TDS), a popular measure for the amount of solid materials dissolved into a water source. The Tea Association of the United States recommends using water with 50 – 150 ppm total dissolved solids to brew the best tea. However, this is not a reliable means for measuring mineral content; TDS is a measure of the total amount of solids that are dissolved in water, regardless of what those solids may be.

Some filtration systems will remove all minerals from water, after which specific minerals are added back in, usually some combination of Magnesium, Calcium, Potassium and Sodium. Each of these minerals are responsible for a portion of the taste in the cup. Unfortunately, the chemistry of how these minerals affect the solubility and dissolution of tea compounds is very complex and not yet fully understood.

Hardness

Water hardness refers to the amount of Calcium and Magnesium dissolved into a water supply. There are two types of hardness: temporary hardness and permanent hardness.

Temporary hardness refers to the presence of Calcium and Magnesium bicarbonates in the water. When in excess, these minerals are known to dull the color of a tea infusion and promote the creation of tea scum. Tea scum is a nasty looking iridescent surface film that will cling to the side of your glass as you drink. Tea scum is caused by the complexation of tea compounds with Calcium Bicarbonate. Temporary hardness can be removed by boiling, but in doing so, it is converted to permanent hardness.

Permanent hardness refers to Calcium and Magnesium carbonates in water; typically water softeners will dissolve these minerals with sodium. Permanent hardness can lead to the deposit of mineral scale in your kettle or water boiler and can result in a stronger, darker brew. It is worth noting that the *Langelier Index* is a tool that can be used in conjunction with proper filtration to produce a water source that will not deposit scale or cause damage to water heating equipment, but the mechanics of the Langelier Index are beyond the scope of this book.

PH LEVEL

The pH level of water is not a huge concern when finding a water source for your tea. pH levels in tap water typically fall within the EPA's recommended pH range of 6.5 – 8.5, and any level within that range is fine for tea. A neutral pH is 7. Water with a pH higher than 7 is considered *basic* or *alkaline*; use of alkaline water will result in a darker tea infusion and a quicker degradation of tea catechins.[1] Water with a pH lower than 7 is considered *acidic* and will result in a lighter tea infusion.

CHOOSING A WATER SOURCE

Regardless of your source, the easiest way to be sure that your water is okay for tea preparation is to smell it and taste it. If it is free from odors and unusual tastes, then you may be good to go. Those earnestly searching for a perfect cup of tea will try multiple water sources; you'll never know how good your tea can be until you try it!

Tap Water

Depending on where you live, tap water can be a great source of water for tea or a terrible source of water for tea. If you are using tap water from a municipal source that has been treated with chlorine, it will affect the taste of the tea. Water that smells and tastes like a swimming pool will produce tea that smells and tastes like a swimming pool! You can remove most of the chlorine in water by boiling it, allowing it to sit in an open container for 24 hours, and/or by filtering it with activated charcoal. Many municipalities have begun replacing chlorine with chloramine, which is not as easy to remove as chlorine. To remove chloramine, you will need to use a special catalytic carbon filter.

If your household's water source is a well, hardness levels are usually the main issue. I recommend filtering all tap water with an activated carbon filter; pitcher-style filters are widely available, and most of them on the market today will remove any funky smells and tastes from water. For most water types, a simple carbon filter will do the job. The goal is not to filter out *all* of the naturally-occurring minerals in your water; many minerals in tap water are useful for a proper infusion and desired taste.

Bottled Spring Water

Bottled spring water is extremely environmentally unfriendly, so I recommend using bottled water only as a last resort. Luckily, there isn't a noticeably huge difference between good filtered tap water and bottled spring water when steeping tea.

When purchasing bottled water, be sure that it is indeed spring water as many bottled waters on the market are merely bottled municipal tap water. Why spring water? Natural springs have a balance of minerals in them, making them ideal for tea preparation. All spring waters contain different levels of different minerals, so it is best to experiment to find one that properly compliments your teas. Just be sure to steer clear of distilled water; this type of water is completely free of minerals and thus tastes dull and flat. Mineral water should also be avoided, as it will often have too high of a mineral content for tea.

chapter 15

Steeping Variables

SURFACE AREA OF TEA LEAVES

The surface area of tea leaves refers to the total area of
the exterior surface of the leaves. For example, let's take
five grams of two finished teas: *Sample A* is a broken-
leaf black tea, and *Sample B* is a full-leaf, unbroken
black tea. Even though we have five grams of both
Sample A and *Sample B*, the surface area of *Sample A*
is greater than that of *Sample B* because it has more
exposed leaf parts due to its broken nature. When
steeped, *Sample A* will have a higher area in contact
with water, allowing for more soluble compounds to dissolve into the water at the same time. This means that
when steeping a tea that has a high surface area (such
as Sample A), you will achieve a beverage of desired
strength faster than you would with a tea with a lower
surface area (Sample B).

RATIO OF TEA LEAVES TO WATER

The amount of tea leaves used during steeping affects the strength of the tea liquor. Adding more leaves to the same amount of water increases the overall surface area of the tea, literally making more tea compounds available for dissolution. As many tea drinkers know, the fastest way to achieve a stronger brew is to steep more tea leaves. However, you can still reach a beverage of desired strength with a smaller amount of leaves; it will simply require a longer steeping time.

STEEPING TIME

Steeping time refers to the amount of time the leaves are in contact with water—the amount of time that dissolution can occur. If given enough time, some compounds in the tea leaves would reach equilibrium, meaning that the concentration of these compounds in the leaves would be the same as the concentration of the same compounds in the water. This wouldn't necessarily make for a palatable infusion, so we adjust the steep time to control the concentration of the compounds in our cup.

WATER TEMPERATURE

Temperature is related to kinetic energy. Increasing the water temperature increases the kinetic energy among the water molecules, allowing them to more effectively dissolve solute molecules. Thus, an increase in water temperature increases the rate of dissolution of soluble compounds in tea leaves. The solubility of various teas peaks at different temperatures; the chemical composition of a cup of tea steeped at different temperatures will vary, sometimes greatly, and so will its taste. In the case of solids, solubility increases and the rate of dissolution increases as the water temperature increases.

STEEPING VESSEL
The kinetics of steeping work irrespective of the vessel that the steeping occurs in. However, when choosing a vessel, there are two things that you must take into consideration:

1. How much heat will the vessel absorb away from your water?
2. Do you have a way to quickly separate the leaves from the water to halt the steeping process?

After you have poured your hot water into a steeping vessel, the temperature can quickly decrease. Depending on the mass of your vessel and the thermoconductivity of its material, the temperature of tea can decrease up to fifteen degrees after thirty seconds. However, this effect can be greatly reduced by preheating the vessel. To preheat your vessel, simply fill it with water at or slightly above the desired steep temperature. Next, let it sit for thirty seconds and decant the water. Preheating reduces the decrease of temperature after thirty seconds by half.

Second, it is important that you are able to quickly separate the leaves from the water to halt the steeping process. The simplest way to halt the steeping process is to decant the vessel's contents through a strainer. Some steeping vessels are equipped with a built-in strainer that can be removed once steeping is complete.

RELATIONSHIP BETWEEN TIME AND TEMPERATURE

When steeping tea, the results of water temperature and steep time on our beverage are inversely correlated. This means that if you have a *preferred* steep time and water temperature that you use to prepare an infusion of a particular strength, slightly increasing the steep time and decreasing the water temperature will yield a similar result. Likewise, decreasing the steep time and increasing the water temperature will also yield a similar result. I have observed that for each 20 degree rise in steep temperature, you can halve the infusion time. Likewise, for each 20 degree decrease in steep temperature you can double the infusion time and achieve a similar result. Remember though that changing the temperature will alter the solubility of the chemical compounds in the leaves. Higher temperatures can result in cups of tea with differing chemical compositions; while adjusting time can increase or decrease the overall strength of the beverage, adjusting temperature will slightly affect taste.

chapter 16

Putting It All Together

Now that we have a basic understanding of the kinetics of steeping and each of the variables that go into producing a cup of tea, it's time to apply this knowledge. What follows are guidelines that will help you produce a palatable cup of tea. You'll notice I don't go into any depth about fancy steeping equipment—that's because you don't need it. In fact, all that you need to produce a cup of tea are tea leaves, water and a vessel to steep the tea. But because the goal of our discussion is to provide a foundation for better tea preparation, we'll need some *training wheels* for a time:

· A way to measure out small amounts of tea in grams: a small pocket scale is great for this.
· A way to heat water to a specific temperature: this can be an electric kettle with a temperature selection or a stovetop kettle used in conjunction with a digital or instant read thermometer.
· A vessel to steep the tea in and a way to remove the leaves from the vessel. The vessel can be literally

anything that holds water. To remove the leaves, I prefer decanting the water through a strainer into my drinking vessel.

Now that you have acquired your wares, let's begin. We'll start with the ratio of tea to water, or the *dosage*. As a starting point, I recommend using **1 gram for each 50ml of water** for tea preparation. Remember, because styles of tea within a type are processed in a similar manner, their chemical composition is also relatively similar. If you steep similar styles of tea in the same way, it should produce a similar cup. Using the recommended dosage, steep time and temperature from one of the following charts should be a decent starting point for further experimentation.

In each chart you will find a block. These blocks represent a safe zone of both time and temperature given the recommended dosage. To ensure that your tea is steeping at your intended temperature, be sure to preheat all teaware that you will be using prior to steeping so that you maintain that temperature throughout the infusion.

Within each block, a general rule of thumb is that more oxidized teas can withstand hotter steeping temperatures and longer steep times. This is important to note for green teas which, depending on the method of fixing the leaves have gone through, will exhibit a wide range of catechin content. Catechins express themselves in the cup as a bitter taste and astringent mouthfeel. Green teas that were steamed are best prepared using the bottom-left quadrants of the green tea block, while green teas that were pan-fired are best prepared using the top-right quadrants of the green tea block.

GREEN TEA STEEPING CHART

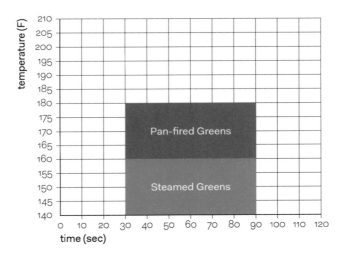

YELLOW TEA STEEPING CHART

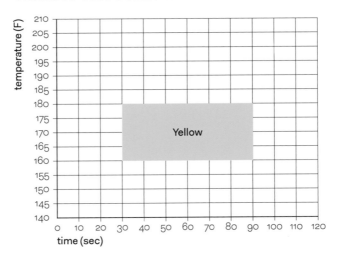

WHITE TEA STEEPING CHART

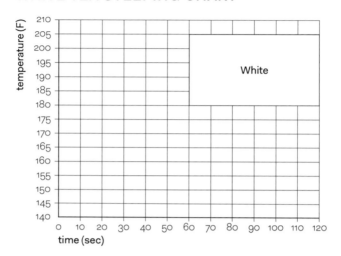

WULONG TEA STEEPING CHART

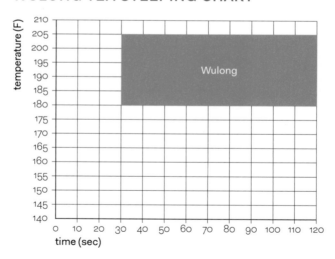

BLACK TEA STEEPING CHART

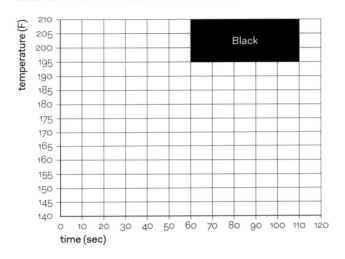

FERMENTED TEA STEEPING CHART

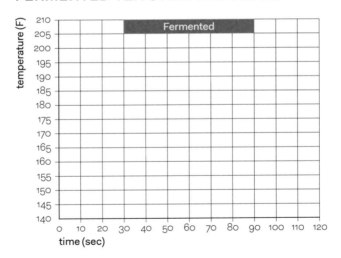

I cannot repeat enough that these charts represent recommended starting points only. Your ideal parameters may vary, especially the steeping time. The amount of time required to produce a beverage of desired strength is greatly dependent upon the surface area of an individual loose tea, and this is something that is not easily measured. Surface area is best determined by sight; it is something that will take time and experience to fully understand. Depending on the tea style that you are steeping, you may be able to achieve more than one infusion. This depends on the dosage, steeping time and temperature, and it is called re-steeping.

MULTIPLE STEEPS

Re-steeping tea is possible when we do not exhaust the flavor potential of the tea in a single steeping. To say it more scientifically, re-steeping is possible when we prevent the chemical components in tea that are responsible for taste, color and body from reaching equilibrium. We can ensure that we're able to re-steep tea by doing two things:

· Increasing the amount of tea leaves we use, which increases the amount of total extractable solids.
· Halting the steeping process by removing the leaves from the water well before equilibrium is reached.

Using the prescribed steeping parameters in this chapter, you can expect to get one to three steeps out of a single dose of leaves. Of course, your mileage will vary based on the type and style of tea being steeped.

Why would one want to steep tea multiple times, you may ask? Multiple steeps allow us to achieve *snapshots* of the tea as dissolution begins, runs it's course, and slowly putters out. As the tea's flavors slowly fade, these snapshots accentuate nuances in the tea that may become muffled during longer infusions. The key is to experiment here; keep adding water and enjoy the tea until the leaves cease to give flavor.

DEVELOPING YOUR PERSONAL STYLE

As you become more comfortable with tea preparation, you will begin to develop your own personal style. You will also notice that some people will hold strong opinions on how to prepare tea. Some of these opinions may seem completely counter to yours; always remember "to each their own!" Some examples of personal styles include: using near boiling water for all teas, dramatically changing steep time for each tea type, or using a large quantity of tea leaves and steeping many, many times.

Preparing Matcha and other Powdered Teas

Matcha and Funmatsucha are two Japanese green teas that are made from tea leaves that have been ground into a very fine powder. These teas are not traditionally steeped. Instead, they are *whisked* into suspension with the water. This is traditionally done with a bamboo tea whisk called a chasen (茶筅) in a bowl called a chawan (茶碗). Typically a special scoop called a chashaku (茶杓) is used to dose two "almond size" scoops of matcha into two to three ounces of 175–180°F water. Each scoop with a chashaku is approximately one gram of tea powder.

TROUBLESHOOTING YOUR TEA

If you are having trouble producing a palatable infusion from your tea, here are a few rules of thumb. For best results, only change one variable at a time and experiment in the order listed.

If your tea is too strong:
· Decrease steep time
· Use less tea
· Decrease steep temperature

If your tea is too weak:
· Increase steep time
· Use more tea
· Increase water temperature

Remember, the *sweet spot* for each tea will vary, so experiment often. Sometimes the best way is to over-steep your tea on purpose, find its limits and then take it back a notch. Tea preparation is not an act governed by strict rules; the methods in this book are simply provided as a starting point for experimentation.

chapter 17

Evaluating Tea

Tea evaluation is a skill that, once learned, can guide more informed tea purchasing (and tea production, if you are a tea producer). We use tea evaluation methods to learn how to describe teas, to compare one tea to another, to give us a vocabulary for easier expansion of our palate and to give us clues about how the tea should be prepared. When evaluating teas, we use our senses of sight, smell, taste and feel along with the knowledge we already have to form an opinion about a tea.

SIGHT
The appearance of finished dry tea leaves, the liquor that they produce, and their appearance when wet can tell us a lot about a particular tea. These details can not only help us to identify a tea, they can also help determine how the tea was processed and handled before it reached our cup.

You will recall that tea types are defined by the processing methods they went through during production, and that oxidation (or the prevention of it) is a major part of processing. One outcome of oxidation is a change in leaf color. Fresh tea leaves begin green, and during oxidation they darken and eventually become a coppery brown color. If oxidation is prevented during processing, they will remain green. Once the tea leaves are dried, they darken slightly. These changes in color are due to a number of chemical changes in the leaves. Chemical changes include the conversion of tea catechins to theaflavins and thearubigins and the degradation of green chlorophylls into black pheophytins.

Some of these color changes translate to liquor color as well; finished tea leaves that appear green typically produce a liquor that is yellow in color, and tea leaves that appear black typically produce a liquor that is red in color. If the amount of oxidation were a scale, green teas would be at the lower end of the scale, followed by yellow teas, then white teas, and then wulong teas. Fermented teas cover a wider range of oxidation and may vary.

Appearance of Finished Tea

The shape and color of finished tea leaves are the strongest indicators of tea type and tea style.

Let's start with tea type. Looking at a finished tea you can quickly discern the amount of oxidation the leaves have gone through and take an educated guess as to what type of tea they represent. There are some grey areas where wulongs are concerned; some wulongs that have gone through minimal oxidation have qualities similar to green teas, and some wulongs that have gone through a large amount of oxidation have qualities similar to black teas.

Down one level in the tea classification hierarchy we have tea styles. As discussed in chapter 5, some tea styles are defined by their appearance and shape. Here are the colors you can expect to see in finished tea leaves, broken down by type:

· Green Tea: dark green to pale green
· Yellow Tea: pale green
· White Tea: silvery white tips, leaves may be anywhere from green to black
· Wulong Tea: green to black
· Black Tea: coppery brown to black
· Fermented Tea: dark green to black

Dry leaf appearance is also an important marker of quality. Tea leaves should reach your hands with minimal breakage. Broken leaves can be a result of machine picking, machine processing, poor handling at origin, poor packaging and shipping, and even poor handling once received. The more broken the tea leaves are, the greater the surface area exposed to water during steeping. This is okay if you are dealing with a broken tea (such as a Darjeeling tea broken and sorted into even particle sizes, or any lower-cost CTC tea), but if your tea is broken into uneven pieces, this is likely due to faulty processing or handling.

Appearance of Tea Liquor

The color of tea liquor is an indicator of the processing steps the leaves endured. The liquor color is also a great timer and indication of the strength of a tea. During oxidation, theaflavins and thearubigins are formed; these chemicals color our cup yellow and red, respectively. Tea pigments change during processing as well and become darker. Green chlorophylls break down into dark pheophytins and tea carotenoids which are made up of yellow xanthophylls and orange carotenes. Here is a breakdown of liquor colors that you can expect to see in steeped tea:

· Green Tea: pale green to bright yellow
· Yellow Tea: varying shades of yellow
· White Tea: pale to bright yellow
· Wulong Tea: huge variance from yellow to red
· Black Tea: varying shades of red
· Fermented Tea: huge variance from yellow to red to black

The color of tea liquor will differ in intensity depending on the steep time. The liquor color darkens during steeping as more soluble compounds exit the leaves and enter the water. As many tea drinkers know, the color intensity of tea liquor is a great indicator of beverage strength.

Appearance of Wet Leaves

Perhaps the most important indicator of tea quality is the appearance of a tea's wet, unfurled leaves after steeping. There are a number of things to look for here:

· Is there evidence of insect damage? Holes and bite marks on tea leaves can be a sign that little or no pesticides were used on the tea plants.
· Is there evidence of machine harvesting? Uneven or broken tea leaves are a sign of machine picking. Also,

bits of woody stem in the tea are a sign that a machine was used to harvest the tea.

· Are the leaf particles uniform? Even if machine harvested, the leaf particles can be uniform from sorting. Uniformity is important in a broken tea to ensure that dissolution of tea compounds occurs at a similar rate across all tea particles while steeping.

· What is the plucking standard of the tea style? With some styles of rolled tea leaves, you won't be able to see how many leaves were plucked to produce the tea until the leaves unfurl. This is especially the case with half-ball style wulongs. Once they unfurl, you may notice that each half-ball shape is made up of 3–5 leaves still attached to a stem.

SMELL

Aroma is a huge portion of our enjoyment of tea. Not only do we use aroma to evaluate dry and wet tea leaves, aroma is also part of the flavor equation when we drink tea. We evaluate the aroma of tea by using our sense of smell or *olfaction* to perceive the volatile compounds that make up tea's aroma complex. There are actually two ways in which we're able to smell tea: orthonasal olfaction and retronasal olfaction.

· Orthonasal olfaction occurs when we inhale odors through our nose. For example, when we open a new bag of tea and smell it or when we smell wet leaves after we've steeped them.

· Retronasal olfaction occurs when we drink tea and the odors within rise up "behind the roof of the mouth and into the nasal cavity"[1]

Volatile aroma compounds from the tea leaves or steeped tea reach our olfactory epithelium and are then perceived by the brain.[2] The average human can discriminate between 10,000 and 40,000 different odors.[3]

TASTE

Taste, or *gustation*, refers to our ability to perceive sensations of bitter, salty, sweet, sour and umami from the chemical components in tea liquor. According to Rachel Herz in her book, "The Scent of Desire,"

> Most people assume that taste is restricted to the tongue, but you actually taste with your whole mouth. Taste buds are located in small pits and grooves called papillae that are on your tongue, the roof of your mouth, your throat, and the insides of your cheeks. What you see on your tongue are the papillae, not the taste buds. Each papilla has a number of taste buds in it—the average number is about six—and within each taste bud there are forty to sixty taste cells, arranged in segments like an orange. The tongue itself contains about five thousand taste buds. All the taste regions in your mouth combined contain approximately ten thousand taste buds.[4]

Certain compounds in tea can be tied directly to taste. They are:

· Bitter: methylxanthines, namely caffeine, theobromine and theophylline
· Bitter: polyphenols, specifically, catechins
· Umami: amino acids
· Sweet: carbohydrates

It it important to note that the taste profile of a tea will differ with changes in liquor temperature.

MOUTHFEEL

Mouthfeel refers to the sensation of tea in the mouth, and mouthfeel makes up part of the flavor equation along with aroma and taste. Tea liquor can have varying levels of viscosity; it can even produce a drying sensation on the tongue known as *astringency*. Common words used to describe the mouthfeel of tea include:

Astringent	Roundy	Unctuous
Buttery	Silky	Velvety
Creamy	Smooth	Watery
Oily	Structured	
Robust	Thick	

FLAVOR

In the world of tea, *taste* and *flavor* are two different attributes of a tea. Tea flavor refers to our combined understanding of a tea after processing its taste, mouthfeel, and smell. Each person may process and interpret flavors differently, but we can use a common language to describe them. Flavor charts or flavor wheels are common tools used to help us put words to our flavor sensations. It is also helpful to note levels of intensity along with the flavor you are experiencing. Here is a tool for describing tea flavors:

TEA FLAVORS

ANIMAL

Game

Leather

Manure

Musk

Wet Fur

CHAR

Ash

Burnt Food

Burnt Toast

Fireplace

Grilled Food

Roasted Nuts

Smoke

Tar

Toast

Tobacco

FLORAL

Cherry Blossom

Dandelion

Gardenia

Geranium

Honeysuckle

Hops

Jasmine

Lavender

Lilac

Orange Blossom

Orchid

Osmanthus

Perfume

Rose

MARINE

Fish

Sea Air

Seaweed

MINERAL

Brass

Flint

Metallic

Salt

Wet Stones

NUTTY

Almond

Chestnut

Grain

Hazelnut

Peanut

Rice

Roast Nuts

Walnut

SPICE

Cardamom

Cinnamon

Clove

Cocoa

Licorice

Nutmeg

Pepper

Vanilla

SWEET

Burnt Sugar

Candy

Caramel

Chocolate

Honey

Malt

Maple Syrup

Molasses

Nectar

Toffee

SOAP

Bar soap

EARTHY

Earth
Barnyard
Compost
Decaying Wood
Dirt
Forest Floor
Moss
Mushroom
Musty
Peat
Wet Earth
Wet Leaves

Wood
Bark
Camphor
Cedar
Cherry Wood
Fresh Cut Wood
Green Wood
Hard Wood
Maple
Pine
Resin/Sap
Sawdust
Wet Wood

FRUIT

Berry
Blackberry
Blackcurrant
Raspberry
Strawberry

Citrus
Citrus Zest
Grapefruit
Lemon
Lime
Orange

Dried Fruit
Fig
Prune
Raisin
Lime
Orange

Tree Fruit
Apricot
Cherry
Fig
Green Apple
Muscatel/Grape
Peach
Pear
Plum
Red Apple

Tropical
Banana
Lychee
Longan
Mango
Melon
Pineapple

VEGETAL

Bitter	Brassica	Grass	Herbal
Arugula	Broccoli	Bamboo	Cardamom
Chard	Brussels Sprouts	Barnyard	Coriander
Collard Greens	Cabbage	Fresh Cut Grass	Dill
Endive	Cauliflower	Grass Seed	Eucalyptus
		Stems	Fennel Seed
		Straw / Hay	Mint
			Parsley
			Saffron
			Thyme

Leafy Green	Root Vegetable	Stem Vegetable
Chard	Carrot	Asparagus
Kale	Daikon	Celery
Lettuce	Radish	Kohlrabi
Spinach	Yam	Rhubarb

chapter 18

Storing the Leaves

Storing tea can be very simple. If you keep your tea in
an airtight container and then store your container in
a dark, cool, dry place free from strong odors, you will
likely consume it before any degradation in aroma or
taste occurs. However, tea is constantly deteriorating,
very slowly, as soon as the leaves are picked off the plant.

When we talk about a tea deteriorating, we are mostly talking about oxidation. Teas that are prevented from
oxidizing during production and teas that are not heavily
oxidized during processing will continue to oxidize over
time. Because these teas are typically prized for their
vitality and lack of oxidation, this ongoing oxidation is
considered a harmful form of deterioration. This is the
case for green teas, yellow teas and some white teas.

For teas that are allowed to oxidize during production, especially those that are purposely heavily
oxidized, there is much less potential for oxidation to
continue. If it does, further oxidation of these teas is
much harder to notice in the cup. This is the case for
black teas and heavily oxidized wulongs.

STORING TEA TO BE AGED

What about aged teas? Isn't that a special case for tea storage? In short, yes. The goal of aging a tea is to allow the tea to change over time in order to increase its palatability. The way in which these teas are aged depends on how we store them; aging tea is synonymous with storing tea.

Hermetic Seal Storage

When teas are stored in an airtight vessel, the ambient oxygen left in the container allows the tea to slowly oxidize over time. Wulong teas are typically sealed in a container with an airtight seal, and they are often left to age for many years.

Non-Hermetic Seal Aging

Puer (and other fermented teas) are not typically shielded from moisture. Instead, a controlled level of moisture is employed to influence the aging during storage. In this case, over time, the tea leaves undergo a combination of fermentation and oxidation. In fact, the raw leaves that become Puer are often fixed at a lower temperature so that the oxidative enzymes within the leaves are not fully denatured. This method of fixing allows for further oxidation at a later stage.

STORING ALL OTHER (NON-AGED) TEAS

So if we're not actively trying to age our tea and we just want to preserve the fresh nature of it, what must we do? There are six laws of tea storage that will help you:

Tea must be kept free from oxygen

Tea leaves continue to oxidize over time with exposure to oxygen. Even when stored in an airtight vessel, some air remains in between the leaves and at the top of the vessel; airtight does not mean air-free.

Some teas come prepackaged in vacuum sealed bags; it is typical for ball-style wulongs to be packaged in this manner. Vacuum sealing is a great way to ensure that the tea leaves are safe for a long time. However, this method can only be used for strong leaves. Vacuum sealing a delicate leaf will crush it! This is why ball-style wulongs are a perfect candidate for vacuum sealing.

For teas that are more delicate, the packages may be flushed with nitrogen while they are sealed. This way, the leaves are not exposed to oxygen and do not degrade over time.

Another option is to use oxygen-absorbing packets that usually contain iron and salt. When placed in an airtight vessel, the remaining oxygen oxidizes the iron, creating rust. Once all of the iron has oxidized, the oxygen absorbing packet can no longer absorb oxygen. These packets are really only good for long term storage; opening and closing the container will keep letting oxygen in, rendering the packet useless after a short time.

Tea must be kept free from heat

Low-level heat speeds up oxidation, while high levels of heat prevent oxidation. Some delicate green and yellow teas are best if stored in the freezer or refrigerator; the cold temperatures dramatically slow down oxidation reactions. However, this must be done properly to avoid condensation on the leaves.

It is advisable to re-package the tea into small packets so that your supply overall will stay fresher for longer. Each packet should be used within a week after opening. Before you put the packages in the freezer, squeeze as much air out as possible; any remaining air will condense and cause moisture to develop on the leaf surface. The most important thing to remember when using cold storage for teas is that when you remove a packet from the freezer or refrigerator, do not open it until it has reached room temperature. This will prevent any condensation from occurring as the leaves come up to room temperature.

Tea must be kept away from light
Much of what is written on the effects that light has on dry tea leaves is based on anecdotal evidence; this topic hasn't been studied in depth. We do know that light-induced damage gives tea a metallic flavor. While tea aficionados are still figuring out exactly what chemical changes are occurring in the leaves, it's wise to keep your tea free from light.

Tea must be kept away from strong odors
Tea leaves will absorb the scents of their surroundings. This is beneficial in the production of scented teas, such as jasmine; the leaves are stored in close proximity to jasmine blossoms, resulting in a jasmine scented tea. However, this same quality of tea can be detrimental should your tea leaves come in contact with unpleasant odors. This not only means that you should store your

tea storage vessels in a place free from strong smells, it also means that whatever you are storing your tea in must not have a strong smell itself. Certain wooden containers, airtight tins with strong-smelling rubber seals, and plastic containers can all leave your tea with a disagreeable aroma and taste.

Tea must be kept away from moisture

It's no secret that tea leaves release their flavor when exposed to moisture. Because of this, you really don't want your tea to "steep" until you steep it for drinking. Keeping your tea storage free of moisture isn't as simple as keeping the leaves away from visible liquids. Tea is *hygroscopic*, meaning that it will absorb moisture from the air. An airtight storage container is the simplest way to block out moisture.

Tea is best when stored in bulk

This is basically a combination of the first and fourth rules above, but it is worth mentioning. A near empty airtight vessel with a tiny bit of tea in the bottom will deteriorate faster than an airtight vessel completely full of tea. To keep your tea the freshest, fill your storage vessel as much as possible, shake it to let the tea settle, and then fill it some more. The more tea you can keep in an enclosed space, the less oxygen there will be in that space. Less air will make it harder for the tea to absorb the smells of its surroundings. This concept is of utmost importance when aging Puer and other fermented teas; you want a closet that smells like tea, not a few teas that smell like your closet.

PRO TIPS

Teas that are less oxidized (greens, yellows and whites) degrade more quickly than teas that are more oxidized (wulongs and blacks).

The more broken the leaves are, the higher the surface area in contact with air. More broken leaves will deteriorate faster.

When taking tea from its original package and putting it into your own container, always label it clearly with the type of tea, style of tea, where you purchased it and when. I can't count how many times I've discovered a random tin of "miscellaneous tea" around the house. This is also helpful for going back through your collection and seeing how your tastes change over time.

If you buy tea in bulk for personal consumption, consider repackaging it into small amounts that can be unsealed as you go. Many tea merchants sell their tea in foil-lined zip seal bags; these can come in handy because they are available in many sizes and are easy to label.

Call to Action

View the changelog at: www.worldoftea.org/changelog

Tony is available for speaking and consulting in the tea space. Contact him at: tony@worldoftea.org

Photography Note

In chapters 6–12, the tea leaf and liquor photos were taken with a Canon 5D Mark II using a 50mm prime lens set to f16, 1/125, ISO 200.

The tea liquors were prepared using the ISO 3103 steeping method wherein 2 grams of tea are steeped in 208°F water for 6 minutes (this method is often called the *trial by fire* method). The water used for the liquors was Volvic Natural Spring Water from Clairvic Spring in Volvic France. The water has a pH of 7 and a TDS of 130 PPM. Specifically, the mineral composition in mg/l is: Calcium 12, Sulfates 9, Magnesium 8, Potassium 6, Silica 32, and Chlorides 15.

The cups that held the leaves and liquor hold 20 cubic centimeters of water, are 2.6 cm high and have a diameter of 4 cm.

Acknowledgments

To those that helped me as I embarked on my tea journey and the many friends I've made along the way.

David Barenholtz
Dan Bolton
Ricardo Caicedo
Cindy Chen
Derek Chew
Roy Chiu
Chicco Chou
Ian Chun
Michael J Coffey
Daniel Coniglio
Emilio Jose Del Pozo
Stéphane Erler
Roy Fong
Tyler Fry
Gabriel Furnari
Kevin Gascoyne
Katie Gebely

Gregory Glancy
Eric Glass
Jordan G. Hardin
Danielle Hochstetter
Austin Hodge
Zhuping Hodge
The Ino Family
Chris Kornblatt
Sonam Lama
Rajiv Lochan
Vivek Lochan
Matthew London
Peter Luong
Nigel Melican
Mina Park
Lew Perin
Elyse Petersen

Lainie Petersen
Wang Pin
James Norwood Pratt
Dan Robertson
Shiv Saria
Eric Scott
Gingko Seto
Imen Shah
Thomas Shu

Thomas Smith
Shiuwen Tai
Bill and Janet Todd
Hiroyuki Unno
Jason Walker
Hongyao Wang
Scott Wilson
Richard Zhang
Vee-vee Zhang

Notes

HOW TO USE THIS BOOK

1. For an in-depth genealogy of words for tea, see Appendix C in Mair and Hoh's *True History of Tea*. (Thames & Hudson)

THE BASICS

TEA GROWING & HARVESTING

1. In China and Taiwan, it is believed that Da Ye Zhong (大叶种) or *big leaf variety* refers to descendants of the *assamica* variety and Xiao Ye Zhong (小叶种) or *small leaf variety* refers to descendants of the *sinensis* variety.
2. Francis Zee, Dwight Sato, Lisa Keith, Peter Follet, and Randall T. Hamasaki, "Small-scale Tea Growing and Processing in Hawaii" (Hilo: College of Tropical Agriculture and Human Resources, 2003), 4.
3. Tocklai, *Tea Agronomy in Northeast India* (Kolkata: Purple Peacock Books & Arts Private Limited, 2011).
4. "FAOSTAT Gateway," Food and Agriculture Organization of the United Nations, http://faostat3.fao.org/home/index .html.

5. William H. Ukers, "All About Tea" (New York: The Tea and Coffee Trade Journal Company, 1935), vol. 1, 268.
6. "FAOSTAT Gateway."

CHEMICAL COMPOSITION OF TEA LEAVES

1. N Kuhnert, JW Drynan, J Obuchowicz, MN Clifford, M Witt, "Mass Spectrometric Characterization of Black Tea Thearubigins Leading to an Oxidative Cascade Hypothesis for Thearubigin Formation," *Rapid Communications in Mass Spectrometry* 24, 23 (2010), 3387–3404.
2. "Tea Cultivation," Tocklai, Accessed October 28, 2012, http://www.tocklai.org/activities/tea-cultivation/.
3. Matthew E. Harbowy and Douglas A. Balentine, "Tea Chemistry," *Critical Reviews in Plant Sciences* 16, 5 (1997), 415–80.
4. Sezai Ercisli, Emine Orhan, Ozlem Ozdemir, Memnune Sengul and Neva Gungor, "Seasonal Variation of Total Phenolic, Antioxidant Activity, Plant Nutritional Elements, and Fatty Acids in Tea Leaves Grown in Turkey," *Pharmaceutical Biology* 46 (2008), 683–87.
5. I.S. Bhatia, "Composition of Leaf in Relation to Liquor Characteristics of Made Tea," *Two and a Bud* 8, 3 (1961), 11–14.
6. Helen Potter, "Uncovering the Secrets of Tea," *Royal Society of Chemistry*, November 14, 2012, http://www.rsc.org/chemistryworld/2012/11/tea-health-benefits.
7. Wei-Wei Deng, Yue Fei, Shuo Wang, Xiao-Chun Wan, Zheng-Zhu Zhang, and Xiang-Yang Hu, "Effect of Shade Treatment on Theanine Biosynthesis in Camellia Sinensis Seedlings," *Plant Growth Regulation* 71, 3 (2013), 295–99.
8. Harbowy and Balentine, 426.
9. Victor R. Preedy, "Tea in Health and Disease Prevention," (London: Academic Press, 2012), 383.
10. "Tea Chemistry," Tocklai, Accessed October 28, 2012, http://www.tocklai.org/activities/tea-chemistry/.

11. Harbowy and Balentine, 426.
12. Yu Long Chen, Jun Duan, Yue Ming Jiang, John Shi, Litao Peng, Sophia Xue and Yukio Kakuda, "Production, Quality, and Biological Effects of Oolong Tea (Camellia Sinensis),"*Food Reviews International* 27, 1 (2010), 5.
13. Yong-Su Zhen, "Tea: Bioactivity and Therapeutic Potential," (London: Taylor & Francis, 2002), 5.
14. Zhen, 68.
15. Zhen, 68.
16. Tea has been labeled the cause of fluorosis in Tibet where excessive amounts of hei cha are consumed. Hei Cha is often made from older leaves on the tea plant which contain higher levels of fluorine.
17. Preedy, 308.
18. Tocklai, "Tea Chemistry."

TEA PROCESSING

1. S.B. Deb, "A Resume on Withering Experiments from the Biochemistry View Point," *Two and a Bud* 13, 2 (1966), 35–41.
2. Specifically when polyphenols in the cell's vacuoles and the peroxidase in the cell's peroxisomes mix with polyphenol oxidase in the cell's cytoplasm. From Michael Harney's 2008, "The Harney and Sons Guide to Tea."
3. In Latin, *flavus* means yellow.
4. In Latin, *rubugin* means red.
5. R.P. Basu and M.R. Ullah, "Notes on Tea Fermentation," *Two and a Bud* 25, 1 (1978), 7–11.
6. In semi-oxidized teas, specifically wulongs, a common descriptor used is "percentage of oxidation." In most cases, this will be an estimated percentage unless the tea is produced on a commodity scale where chemical tests are performed to reveal the actual percentage of oxidation by way of catechin or theaflavin and thearubigin content.

7. In China, this is referred to as *chao qing* (炒青), literally, "firing the green."
8. In China, this is referred to as *zheng qing* (蒸青), literally, "steam green."
9. In China, this is referred to as *sha qing ji* (杀青机), literally, "kill green machine."
10. In China, this is referred to as *hong qing* (烘青), literally, "baked green"
11. A food product that is shelf-stable is one that has been processed so that it can be safely stored at room temperature for an extended period of time, known as its *shelf-life.*
12. In South Korea, this is referred to as an *ondol* (온돌), or "heated floor."
13. Tocklai, "Drying," Accessed October 28, 2012, http://www.tocklai.net/activities/tea-manufacture/drying/.
14. K. C. Wilson and M. N. Clifford, "Tea Cultivation to Consumption," (Netherlands: Springer, 1992), 439.

TEA CLASSIFICATION

GREEN TEA

1. Liang Chen, Zeno Apostolides, and Zong-Mao Chen, "Global Tea Breeding Achievements," (Hangzhou: Zhejiang University Press, 2012), 229–234.
2. Zee, "Small-scale Tea Growing and Processing in Hawaii."
3. Liang Chen, "Global Tea Breeding Achievements," 2.
4. "Patent CN101006808A – Technique for Processing Bead Tea,"Google Patents, Accessed February 1, 2014, http://www.google.com/patents/CN101006808A.
5. Austin Hodge, "About Tai Ping Hou Kui," *Seven Cups* (blog), 2014, https://sevencups.com/learn-about-tea/famous-chinese-tea/about-tai-ping-hou-kui/.
6. Gingko Seto, "Bamboo Leaf Green, Trademarks and Lawsuits of Teas," *Life in Teacup* (blog), 2011, http://

gingkobay.blogspot.com/2011/04/bamboo-leaf-green-trade
marks-and.html.

YELLOW TEA

1. Nigel Melican, comment on World of Tea, "Balhyocha
   & Hwancha," 2013, http://www.worldoftea.org/
   south-korean-balhyocha-hwangcha/#comment-11744.
2. Austin Hodge, "Yellow Tea – Seven Cups Fine Chinese
   Teas," *Seven Cups* (blog), 2009, http://www.sevencups.com/
   about-tea/yellow-tea/.

WHITE TEA

1. You'll often read that white tea is not oxidized. This is
   because it is not intentionally oxidized like black tea or
   wulong. Instead, it is oxidized as a result of a long withering period during production.
2. Mary Lou Heiss and Robert J. Heiss, "The Story of Tea,"
   (Berkeley: Ten Speed Press, 2007).
3. Statistic provided by Cha Dao Life Magazine, Issue 1, "The
   Four Classes of White Tea."

WULONG TEA

1. Liang Chen, "Global Tea Breeding Achievements," 18.
2. Jason C.S. Chen, "A Tea Lover's Travel Diary: Phoenix
   Single-Tree Oolong Tea and Tie Kian Yin Oolong Tea,"
   (C.C. Fine Tea, 2010).
3. Austin Hodge, "Wu Yi Yan Cha," *Seven Cups* (blog), 2009,
   http://www.sevencups.com/tea-culture/famous-chinese-tea/
   da-hong-pao-big-red-robe-rock-oolong/.
4. Luo Yingyin, "Taiwan's Green Gold – High Mountain Tea,"
   Art of Tea 13, (2012).

BLACK TEA

1. The broken nature of most Darjeeling black teas is achieved by using pressure on a rolling table.
2. Douglas A. Balentine, Matthew E. Harbowy, and Harold N. Graham, "Tea: The Plant and Its Manufacture; Chemistry and Consumption of the Beverage," in *Caffeine*, edited by Gene A. Spiller. (Boca Raton: CRC Press, 1998), 56.
3. Chen, "Global Tea Breeding Achievements," 18.
4. See this article for the most current thinking on Zheng Shan Xiao Zhong: http://languagelog.ldc.upenn.edu/nll/?p=16145.
5. Chen, "Global Tea Breeding Achievements," 74.
6. "FAOSTAT Gateway;" Chen, "Global Tea Breeding Achievements," 125.
7. Chen, "Global Tea Breeding Achievements," 132.

FERMENTED TEA

1. Chen, "Global Tea Breeding Achievements," 18.
2. For in-depth coverage of the events leading up to the Puer bubble and Puer culture in general, read "Puer Tea, Ancient Caravans and Urban Chic" by Jinghong Zhang.
3. Ian Chun, "Furyu: Batabatacha Rare Bancha Tea," *Yunomi Life*, http://www.yunomi.life/products/furyu-batabatacha-rare-bancha-tea-30g.

ALTERED TEA

1. From a personal communication with Wolfgang Boehmer of Flavor Dynamics Inc.
2. "How Tea is Flavored," Adagio, Accessed February 1, 2016, http://www.teaclass.com/lesson_0201.html.
3. Chen, "Production, Quality, and Biological Effects of Wulong Tea (Camellia Sinensis)."
4. K. C. Wilson and M. N. Clifford, "Tea Cultivation to Consumption," 526.

5. From a personal communication with Daniel Coniglio of AIYA America, Inc.
6. Steven Owyoung, "A Primer on Ddok Cha," *Cha Dao* (blog), 2009, http://chadao.blogspot.com/2008/08/primer-on-ddok-cha.html.

ENJOYING TEA

KINETICS OF STEEPING
1. It is important to note that this is an oversimplification and that each chemical component within tea leaves will dissolve and diffuse at different rates and that the concentrations of each will differ.

WATER QUALITY
1. Shengmin Sanga, Joshua D. Lambert, Chi-Tang Ho, and Chung S. Yang, "The Chemistry and Biotransformation of Tea Constituents, *Pharmacological Research* 64 (2011), 92.

EVALUATING TEA
1. Rachel Herz, *The Scent of Desire: Discovering Our Enigmatic Sense of Smell* (Harper Perennial, 2008), Kindle Edition, Location 2526.
2. Herz, *The Scent of Desire*, Location 517.
3. Herz, *The Scent of Desire*, Location 425.
4. Herz, *The Scent of Desire*, Location 2390.

Appendix

CHINA'S TEN MOST FAMOUS TEAS

	TEA NAME	CHINESE	PINYIN	TYPE
1	Xi Hu Long Jing	西湖 龙井	xī hú lóng jǐng	Green Tea
2	Dong Ting Bi Luo Chun	洞庭 碧螺春	dòng tíng bì luó chūn	Green Tea
3	Huang Shan Mao Feng	黄山毛峰	huáng shān máo fēng	Green Tea
4	Jun Shan Yin Zhen	君山银针	jūn shān yín zhēn	Yellow Tea
5	Qimen Hong Cha	祁門紅茶	qí mén hóng chá	Black Tea
6	Wu Yi Da Hong Pao	武夷 大红袍	wǔ yí dà hóng páo	Wulong Tea
7	Lu An Gua Pian	六安瓜片	lù ān guā piàn	Green Tea
8	Anxi Tie Guan Yin	安溪 铁观音	ān xī tiě guān yīn	Wulong Tea
9	Tai Ping Hou Kui	太平猴魁	tài píng hóu kuí	Green Tea
10	Xin Yang Mao Jian	信阳 毛尖	xìn yáng máo jiān	Green Tea

Index

Lightning Source UK Ltd.
Milton Keynes UK
UKIC03n1529121216
289809UK00006B/5

* 9 7 8 0 9 9 8 1 0 3 0 0 6 *